CORINTH
MYCENAE
TIRYNS NAUPLION

TEXT AND PHOTOGRAPHS
BY SPYROS MELETZIS
AND HELEN PAPADAKIS

VERLAG SCHNELL & STEINER MUNICH · ZURICH
ART EDITIONS MELETZIS & PAPADAKIS · ATHENS

Text and photographs by Spyros Meletzis and Helen Papadakis. English translation by Paul J. Dine, M. — The front cover shows the Temple of Apollo at Corinth, and the back cover a detail of the " Warrior Vase ", found at Mycenae, now in the National Museum, Athens. This vase has also been the model for the ornament on p. 17 over the text on Mycenae.

Abbreviations

a. Chr. = ante Christum natum = before Chr.
p. Chr. = post Christum natum = after Chr.
s. = saeculum = century
NMA = National Museum of Athens

4th edition 1981   ISBN 3 7954 0590 4
SOLE DISTRIBUTOR FOR GREECE: HELEN PAPADAKIS, 15 PEFKON ST., ATHENS 625
VOLUME 69/70 IN THE SERIES "GROSSE HUNSTFÜHRER" (ART GUIDES) OF OUR PUBLISHING HOUSE GENERAL EDITORS OF THE SERIES: DR. HUGO SCHNELL AND DR. PAUL MAI, AND FOR THE VOLUMES ON GREECE DR. JOHANNES STEINER. – © 1976 BY VERLAG SCHNELL & STEINER GMBH CO., MUNICH - ZURICH. PRINTED BY KINA ITALIA, MILANO AND BY SCHNELL & STEINER WALDSASSEN (BAYERN)

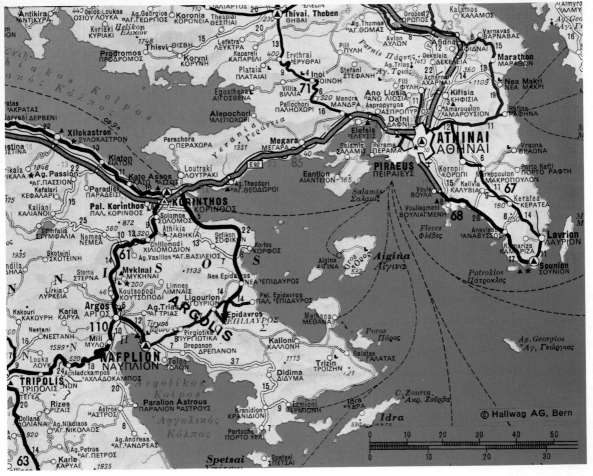

Situation: Argolis–Attica

ARGOLIS
AND THE REGION AROUND CORINTH

The Isthmus of Corinth separates the Peloponnesus from Attica. The Argolis-Corinth region is the part of the Peloponnesus that extends furthest to the east: a peninsula that juts out into the Aegean Sea. To the north-east, on the other side of the Saronic Gulf and the island of Aegina, lies Attica with its " riviera ", through which one passes when one drives from Athens along a magnificent highway to Cape Sunium. In the south and south-west, it is bounded by the Gulf of Argolis and in the north it fringes on the Corinthiacus, the Gulf of Corinth. High mountain ranges divide it from Arcadia to the west, ranges that tend to converge further south: the northernmost mountain is Cyllene or Ziria (7816 ft.), where, as legend tells us, Hermes was born; progressing south, we pass mounts Oligyrtus, Trachy, Lyrchion, Artemisium (5832 ft) and finally Ktenias, along the ridge of which the road connecting Argos with Tripolis was built. From it one has a splendid view of both the entire plain and the Gulf of Argolis.

3

The *coast of Argolis* begins at Lerna and curves round like a sickle to Nauplia on the other side. The rich green of the fertile coastal strip blends in gentle harmony with the turquoise hue of the waters in which Palamidi, Nauplia's citadel, and the nearby islet of Bourtzi are mirrored. There are two great plains on this mountainous peninsula: that of Argolis to the south and of Corinth to the north; the two are connected by the narrow pass of Dervenakia.

Mount Arachnaion (3946 ft) severs the plain of Argolis from the remainder of the peninsula to the east. On its summit the fire was kindled that carried the news of the Greek victory at Troy to the Mycenaeans.

East of this bare and rocky mountain range lies *Epidaurus,* where according to the local legend the great god of healing Asclepius (Aesculapius) was born on Mount Tition. In mythical times the landscape around Corinth and the plain of Argolis was the hub and centre of Greece and of Mycenaean civilization and culture. The focal point was Mycenae around which were clustered small and larger towns like Tiryns, Midea or Dendra, Prosymna, Berbati, Argos, Nauplia and Asine, all towns where archaeology has brought rich finds to light, too. It was in this region of such fertile culture that the most interesting, most important and most renowned sagas of the best-known and most-famed heroes of mythical times were created.

Argos is the centre of the legends about Io, the daughter of Inachus, as also of those connected with Danaus and his 50 daughters. Here, too, Perseus was brought forth: he journeyed to the ends of the earth and struck off the Medusa's head; in Ethiopia he slew the sea monster and rescued the king's daughter Andromeda. On Acrocorinth, Bellerophon, the Corinthian hero, tamed Pegasus, the winged horse, and, mounted on it, he killed the Chimera, a two-headed monster with a mythical body: a lion-goat with a dragon's tail. It was from Argos that the " Seven against Thebes " went forth, renowned heroes with Adrastus at their head.

It was in this region that Heracles, hero of heroes, carried out his most redoubtable deeds: in Nemea he slew the invulnerable lion, in Lerna the Hydra with the nine heads and at Lake Stymphalus the Stymphalian birds.

On his way from Troezen to Athens, Theseus accomplished his first heroic deed on the Isthmus of Corinth when he made away with the thug Sinis.

Here, too, the Isthmian and the Nemean Games were celebrated, games of pan-Hellenic character like those at Olympia. From the Argolis plain, Agamemnon, the celebrated king of Mycenae, led the Greeks on their campaign against the Trojans.

To these legends of prehistorical times about the best-known heroes of Greece we must add those sagas of the historical age: they tell of the frightful crimes of the royal line of the Atreids, of Thyestes and Atreus who murdered their own offspring, of incest and adultery, of fratricide, uxoricide, viricide and matricide at the royal court of Mycenae, inspiration enough for the poets and painters of all times. Homer was inspired to create the Iliad and the Odyssey; in the works of writers like Hesiod and Pindar we meet the legendary heroes of Argos; and Aeschylus, Sophocles and Euripides found in the sagas of this region the matter of their immortal tragedies — Agamemnon, Iphigenia, Electra and Oresteia. Here, too, artists and sculptors adorned temples and monuments with their pictures and sculptures, drawing their motifs from the lives and deeds of the legendary heroes of Argolis and Corinth.

Whoever comes to visit and experience at first hand the towns and sites of this landscape will find the facts and events of mythical and historical times come flashing unbidden across his mind's eye, but, whereas school-books and mythologies were able to evoke but a dim impression, here his contact with a living scenery will grant him a deeper understanding and a clearer conception of what happened here in days long past.

4

The archaeological sites are eloquent witnesses to the mythical and historical past; their noble and impressive monuments represent all epochs of Greek antiquity.

Mycenae with *Tyrins, Epidaurus* and *Corinth* not only reflect three different eras in this cultural development; each has also left its irradicable stamp on the Greek spirit and on Greek culture.

Mycenaean culture received its first impulses from the Minoan culture on Crete, the cradle of the European spirit. And as Crete slowly but surely declined in importance, the Mycenaeans were ready to take over the decisive role in the further development of Greek culture, not just on the Peloponnesus but throughout the whole of Greece.

The starting-point of all further progress in Greece has to be sought in *the royal house at Mycenae* which, especially during the time of Atreus and his descendants, enjoyed such a position of might and wealth that Homer refers to Mycenae in the Illiad as the " golden " city and to Agamemnon as " king of kings ".

That *Tiryns* never attained the renown and glory of Mycenae and never played a leading role is easily explained since it nearly always stood under Mycenae's influence.

Epidaurus owes its fame and splendour neither to its princes nor to its position as a seapower nor to its colonies. It would undoubtedly have fallen into oblivion in the course of time had it not been so generous a host to the benefactor and healer Asclepius, the god of medicine.

Corinth, again, famous on account of its wealth and the number of its inhabitants — it was the most populous town in Greece in ancient times —, achieved its great renown not because of the altars and temples of its gods, but through commerce and trade: lying as it did at the foot of Acrocorinth it was master of two seas, the Saronic to the east and the Corinthian to the west.

Nowadays there is no difficulty or inconvenience involved in viewing the archaeological sites in Argolis and Corinth. Anyone can visit them, can spend a few hours lost in thought with the heroes and kings of Mycenae, can wonder at the Cyclopean walls, the beehive graves, and the theatre at Epidaurus and then afterwards imbibe the breathtaking beauty of the bays around the Saronic Gulf.

THE ISTHMUS OF CORINTH

If you take the new national highway from Athens, you reach the Isthmus of Corinth in about an hour (50 miles). From the bridge over the Isthmus we can look down on the irregular strip of land that for centuries separated the Saronic from the Corinthian Gulf; today they are connected. It was the Corinthians themselves who first wanted to dig a passage through this stretch of land, not quite four miles in width, in order to both shorten considerably and to render safer a journey from east to west. Periander, tyrant of Corinth, wanted to translate this plan into reality, but the technical difficulties proved insurmountable. Thus it came about that the "diolkos" was constructed.

The d i o l k o s, or " dragway ", was a paved, not-very-straight road, some 4 to 10 yards wide. At its eastern end, on the Saronic Gulf, lay Skinus, whereas at its western end, on the gulf of Corinth, was the town of Poseidonia. The ships were dragged along the grooves in its paving on carts. When ships arrived at one of the two ports of Corinth, they were at first unloaded, so that their cargo could be transported separately. It was then loaded on the ships again at the other end of the diolkos. Admirable as this technological achievement of antiquity was, it was inevitable that it would not be regarded as the final solution. A canal through the Isthmus became a necessity. Many attempted to construct one: Demetrius I of Macedonia or "Poliorcetes" (= Besieger) as he was surnamed, Julius Caesar, Caligula and Nero. The latter proved to be the most determined and himself opened the construction works personally. However, in spite of the large number of workers engaged in the scheme — some 6000, many of whom were prisoners — his efforts were not crowned with success.

After numerous subsequent attempts, the Corinth Canal was at last opened in July, 1893. It is some 4 miles in length and, at the level of the water, roughly 25 yards wide. The water is 26 feet deep; at its highest point, in the centre, it is some 262 feet above sea level.

Obviously, the Canal makes it easier to trade between the west and the Aegean and makes it unnecessary for ships to circumnavigate the whole of the Peloponnesus. It was protected by a fortifying wall. Excavations have brought parts of this wall to light: they date from 480 B. C., the Byzantine period and the years of the wars against the Turks.

THE SANCTUARY OF POSEIDON AND THE ISTHMIAN GAMES

The patron of the Isthmus was the god Poseidon, that of Acrocorinth was Apollo. Any cult or rite connected with the Isthmus was thus dedicated to Poseidon. The sanctuary and the successive temples that were raised here were plundered and destroyed on a number of occasions.

Ruins remain of
a) the Sanctuary of Palaemon, and
b) the Stadium in which the Games were held in his honour and which was situated near his temple.

After the Olympian Games the Isthmian Games were next in importance in classical times. They were staged every two years, in the spring, which means more frequently than the Olympic Games. The victors were crowned with a wreath of fir twigs or of wild celery. It was in this same stadium, incidentally, that Alexander the Great was declared commander in chief of all the Greek forces. It was here, too, that Titus Quintius Flamininus proclaimed Greece independent of Macedonian rule in the year 196 B. C.

CORINTH

Corinth, one of the oldest and most important cities in the whole of Greece, owed its foundation, wealth and development to its favourable situation: lying as it did on the Isthmus between the Peloponnesus and mainland Greece, it not only had firm control of this landstrip in classical times but maintained its hold on it during the wars against the Turks in the 19th century as well. Morever, it was in the happy position of having two harbours, Cenchreae to the east in the Saronic Gulf and Lechaion (Lechaeum) to the west in the Gulf of Corinth. The soil around Corinth was extremely fertile. The water supply too was excellent, since the town, and later its market place, was built near the Peirene Fountain.

MYTH AND HISTORY

The legends spun around Corinth are numerous and striking: just as Athena and Poseidon struggled for the patronage of Athens, so Apollo and Poseidon were rivals for Corinth. In the end, Apollo became lord of Acrocorinth and Poseidon the patron of the Isthmus. Under the patronage of these two gods, the development of the city began. Excavations at Corinth have shown that the town has been inhabited without interruption from neolithic times on.

Its history began with the Dorian migration — Corinth became a Dorian centre. The first king mentioned is Alites. Bacchis, one of his descendants, is the founder of a royal house named after him the Bacchiadae. They reigned over Corinth for 350 years and it is under them that Corinth flourished.

THE GOLDEN AGE OF CORINTH AND ITS LATER DEVELOPMENT

Under the Bacchiadae, Corinth gradually rose to become one of the most important towns in Greece. Its favourable geographical position and the high quality of its products both contributed to its further positive development. The first colonies were founded: Corcyra, Leucas, Syracuse. After the Corinthians were the first to perfect the galley, their fleet was to be seen everywhere in east and west. Furthermore, the famous polychrome Corinthian vases were produced — the first of their kind — in the potteries of Corinth. The products of this unique ceramic art were soon to be found in all the commercial centres of ancient times. Under the Bacchiadae, Corinth had no serious competitor in the commercial world.

In the mid-7th century Corinth attained still greater prosperity under the tyrants, who came to power for a great variety of reasons. After Corinth had been defeated at sea by Corcyra, Kypselos assumed power (657/6 B. C.) and founded a dynasty. It was under him and his successors that Corinth achieved its greatest fame, power and wealth. The town was adorned at this time with splendid edifices and works of art. Kypselos was followed by his son, Periander, one of the Seven Sages of Greece. He it was who commissioned the important technical achievement, the diolkos (cf. introduction), which was in use from the end of the 7th century B. C. on.

It is during the reign of Periander that Corinth extended its influence over the Ionian Sea. Around 650 B. C. Corinthian ceramics were traded almost everywhere. However, the great demand went hand in hand with a decline in quality: the potter worked faster, motifs were repeated, there was less variety of form. The most valuable and beautiful forms at this time were the smallest. Corinthian brass products were also highly regarded and the art of the armourer highly developed. And the Corinthians produced no mean masters in the fields of sculpture, painting and inlay work.

THE DITHYRAMB

It is to Periander that we owe the development of the dithyramb, a song of praise in honour of Dionysus, since it was he who summoned Arion to his court from Lesbos. So it came about that Corinth occupied a special place in the history of European music, because the dithyramb was closely related to the European tradition in music. The dithyramb was at first merely a series of disconnected cries and primitive songs. Arion transformed this into a work of art. This was then further developed at Athens into a new literary form: the tragedy. Legend also has something to say about Arion: he was supposed to have been rescued by a dolphin when sailors attempted to murder him.

Periander is one of the few tyrants about whom we not only hear bad things but also good. He is numbered among the Seven Sages of Greece and quite a few of the measures he adopted were approved by many of his subjects. However, in his private life he was less fortunate. His successor was Psammetichus, who reigned, however, only for three years. He was the last of Kypselos' descendants. After the tyrants, Corinth was ruled over by an enlightened oligarchy. Later still, during

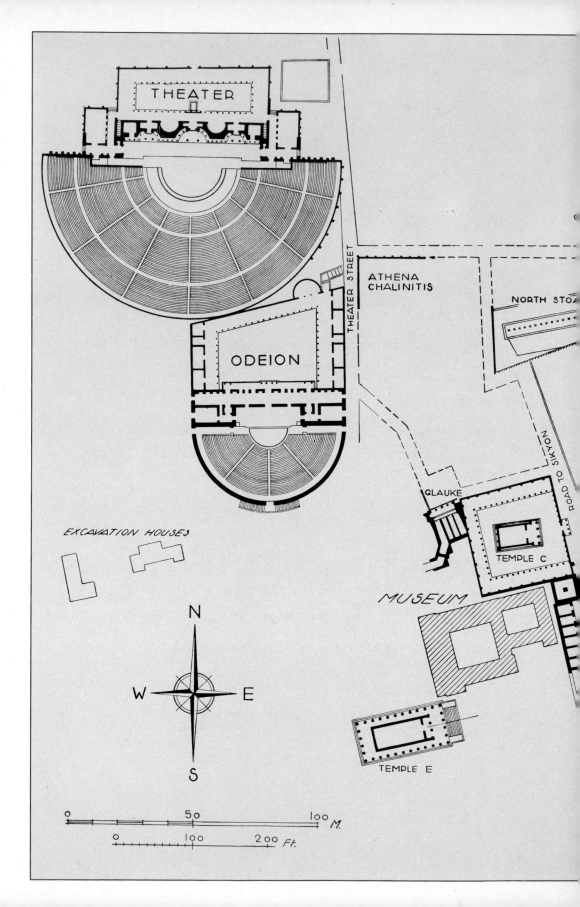

THEATER

ODEION

THEATER STREET

ATHENA
CHALINITIS

NORTH STOA

GLAUKE

ROAD TO SIKYON

TEMPLE C

MUSEUM

TEMPLE E

EXCAVATION HOUSES

N
W   E
S

0   50   100 M.

0   100   200 Ft.

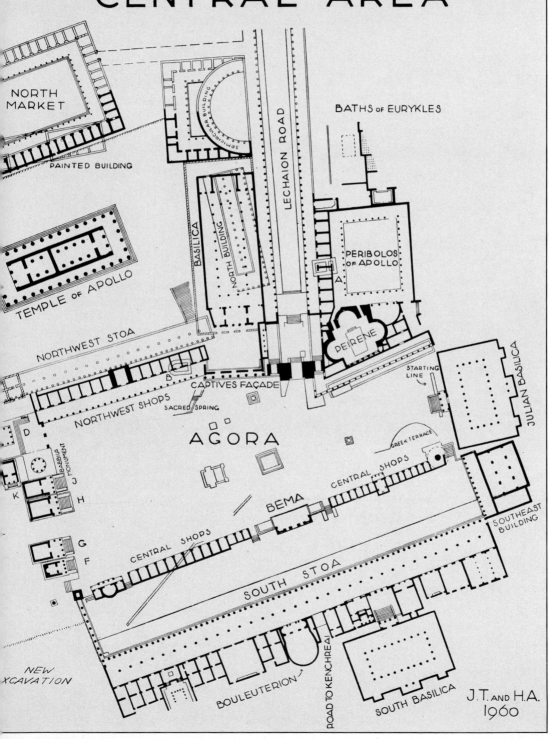

CORINTH
CENTRAL AREA

NORTH MARKET

PAINTED BUILDING

BATHS OF EURYKLES

LECHAION ROAD

SEMICIRCULAR BUILDING

BASILICA

NORTH BUILDING

PERIBOLOS OF APOLLO

A

TEMPLE OF APOLLO

PEIRENE

NORTHWEST STOA

STARTING LINE

B

CAPTIVES FAÇADE

JULIAN BASILICA

NORTHWEST SHOPS

SACRED SPRING

D

AGORA

GREEK TERRACE

BABBIUS MONUMENT

CENTRAL SHOPS

J

BEMA

SOUTHEAST BUILDING

K

H

G

CENTRAL SHOPS

F

SOUTH STOA

NEW XCAVATION

BOULEUTERION

ROAD TO KENCHREAI

SOUTH BASILICA

J.T. AND H.A. 1960

the Persian Wars, the Corinthians fought alongside the Athenians and the other Greeks against the Persians. After the Persian threat had successfully been banned however, Athens became more powerful and vied with Corinth for the supremacy.

MACEDONIANS AND ROMANS

And the more Athens prospered, the more the influence of Corinth declined. The Peloponnesian (431—404 B. C.) and the Corinthian Wars contributed still further to the town's decline.

Then the Macedonians began to win the upper hand in Greece. After the battle of Chaeronea (338 B. C.) Corinth was subjugated by Philip. It was Corinth to which he and later Alexander the Great summoned the Greeks to take part in panhellenic assemblies. This led to a new period of prosperity for Corinth: it was at this time that its inhabitants added to the town's market place the stately south stoa which was hailed as the largest in size on the whole of mainland Greece. Once again, Corinth became a wealthy trading centre, the meeting-place of merchants and travellers. It was also the centre of the cult of Aphrodite. Of the innumerable hetaeras, Lais was the most renowned: her name has gone down in history as a symbol for female beauty and intelligence. Diogenes also lived and taught in the city of Corinth. He was born at Sinope in 413 and died at Corinth in the year 322 B. C. The essence of his teaching and wisdom was: cultivate the simple life.

The time of greatest trial for Corinth came with the last great assault of the Romans on Greece. The year 146 B. C. saw Corinth sacked and totally destroyed. The Roman Consul Lucius Mummius completed his conquest of Greek territories with his victory at Leucopetra: his name will be forever linked with the utter destruction of one of the great cities of antiquity which was renowned for its architecture and its wealth. The inhabitants were either slain or sold as slaves; all Corinth's treasures were shipped off to Rome. For one whole century Corinth was left uninhabited and desolate. It was not until 44 B. C. that Julius Caesar founded the town anew. By reason of its favourable geographical situation Corinth soon attained to new importance and was made the capital of the Roman province of Achaïa.

THE APOSTLE PAUL AT CORINTH

This influential city also aroused the interest of the Apostle Paul. Thus, after his visit to Athens (51—52 AD), he made his way to Corinth, a city whose luxurious sensuality stood in complete contradiction with the precepts of the Christian faith. Paul took a determined stand against the opulent ways of Corinth in his sermons. He remained there for roughly a year. From the first day of his stay there he gathered a crowd of interested hearers around him, both Greeks and Jews. Many of them, like Crispus, the ruler of the synagogue, adopted the new faith. Among the faithful, there were not only humble folk but also people of some substance. As Paul severely censured the way of life of the Corinthians, there was no wonder that his sermons aroused opposition: Paul and his disciples were charged with the introduction of a new religion that set at nought the laws of Moses — as a *Religio Licita* it was already tolerated by the Romans — and cited before the Proconsul, Junius Annaeus Gallio. However, the Proconsul, whose tribune has been excavated in the agora of Corinth, regarded this as an internal affair of the Jews and no concern of the Romans, so that he set Paul free with permission to continue preaching. Thus, it came about that one of the most important of the early Christian communities in Greece was the fruit of his preaching.

Under the Romans a number of stately edifices were erected in Corinth, above all in the Agora. In 67 A. D. Nero made his attempt to pierce the isthmus with a canal. During Vespasian's reign the town was smitten by an earthquake. Emperor Hadrian had splendid new buildings constructed and also built an aqueduct to carry water from Lake Stymphalus to the town. Corinth entered a new period of prosperity. People flocked to the town from all parts and the saying was coined, "It is not granted to everyone to travel to Corinth". Pausanias was in Corinth in 150 A. D. and described what he saw there.

Invasions, conflagrations and terrible earthquakes accompanied Corinth through its history. Often it was totally destroyed and again and again it was rebuilt, sometimes on a larger scale, at other times as a village, right up to the period of the Greek rising against the Turks (1821).

In Byzantine times silk and fine carpets were produced here. In 1146 A. D. Normans had arrived here and brought skilled silk workers with them. Later the Latin Empire extended its sway over Corinth. Leo Sgouros, the courageous defender of Corinth, sprang with his horse from the Acrocorinth to escape capture alive. Corinth remained in Turkish hands until 1822, when it was liberated by the Greek army. The Turkish occupation had been interrupted for a short period of 50 years while the Venetians had the control of the town. As a consequence of its favourable situation, serious consideration was given to making Corinth the capital of liberated Greece. In the end, however, this honour fell to Nauplia.

The town was destroyed by severe earthquakes in 1858; the frightful earthquakes which shattered Corinth in 1928 led to its abandonment by its inhabitants. An entirely new town was constructed down by the sea: New-Corinth, a town safe against the ravages of earthquakes. Where the old town once stood, only a village remained, known as Old-Corinth; and it is just outside its limits that the archaeological site is situated where, year by year, ruins and monuments are laid bare.

TOUR OF THE EXCAVATIONS

Before a start was made with the excavation of the site, the only visible relics of the once great and prosperous Corinth were seven columns of the Temple of Apollo and some of the column bases. Everything else was covered by the earth and dust of centuries. On behalf of the German Archaeological Institute, Dörpfeld first excavated the Temple of Apollo in the year 1886. After him, A. Skiadas of the Greek Archaeological Institute laid bare mainly the walls of the town and part of the Agora. Then, from 1896 on, the American School of Classical Studies at Athens was responsible for the excavations and still continues its work today.

THE ARCHAEOLOGICAL SITE

There are two entrances to the site of the excavations. The one is situated near the village square on the eastern side of the fenced-in area. This leads direct to Lechaion Street. The other entrance is on the west, on the outskirts of the village, near the museum. We shall begin our visit in Lechaion Street.

Lechaion Street (plate 2)

This led straight to Lechaion (Lechaeum), as Pausanias tells us, and thus served as the link between the Agora and Corinth's western harbour, Lechaion, on the Gulf of Corinth (roughly 1.8 miles). From the town fortifications to the harbour (12 stadia / 1.25 miles) the road was protected by long walls not unlike the "long walls" which connected Athens to Piraeus. The road was in use until the 10th century A.D. On the site of the excavations only a little more than 100 yards of Lechaion Street have been laid bare. The road was paved with slabs and was some 8 yards wide, with a pavement for pedestrians on both sides. Numerous bases for statues line either side of the road. Pausanias mentions a whole number of statues which he saw in his day (2nd century A. D.): a seated Hermes with a mountain goat, a Poseidon, a Leucothea, Palaemon on a dolphin and Artemis.

On both sides of the road there was a Roman stoa with Corinthian columns; there were also little quadrangular shops, 16 of them on the western side. Behind the western stoa the remains of a Greek stoa with an outer row of Doric columns and an inner of Corinthian were found — they were destroyed in the year 146 B. C. Again on the western side, behind the Roman stoa, was a terrace where the foundation walls of a large first-century Roman basilica (377 x 213 feet) were found; these had been enlarged in the second century and faced with marble. Beneath the basilica were the remains of a Greek Agora dating from the 5th century B. C.

To the north-west of Lechaion Street traces were uncovered of a semicircular structure on the site of the older Roman Agora. To the left, on the eastern side but more to the north, there are the remains of large baths of the Roman period which have not yet been fully excavated. Perhaps they are the baths of Eurycles which Pausanias informs us were the work of the Spartan Eurycles and the most famous in Corinth, decorated as they were with marble of various colours. Pausanias also tells us that there were baths in many parts of Corinth and numerous springs with an abundance of running water but also that Hadrian had constructed an aqueduct to bring water from Lake Stymphalus.

To the south of the baths there was the garden (peribolos) of Apollo, an unroofed court or enclosure (72 x 92 ft), dating from the 1st century A. D., which was paved with slabs and surrounded by a range of marble columns (peristyle). A few of the columns have been placed upright again.

Perhaps the statue of Apollo mentioned by Pausanias stood in the centre of the peribolos, as did also a painted representation of Odysseus slaying the suitors of Penelope. To the west of the garden, near the road (plan A), the foundation walls of a small Greek temple in the Doric style from the 4th century B. C. have been uncovered.

The Fountain of Peirene (plate 11)

Peirene, the daughter of Achelous, shed so copious tears at the death of her son Cenchrias, who had been accidentally slain by Artemis, that she was metamorphosed into a fountain, or so at least Pausanias tells us (II, 32).

There were two fountains named after Peirene, one high up on the Acrocorinth and the other at the foot of the mountain. The water of the upper fountain was channelled to a large basin near the Peirene Fountain which was hewn out of the rock and subdivided into four. It had a total capacity of some 520 cubic yards. In front of the great basin were 3 containers which were always full so that people could draw water from them. The architecture of the Fountain of Peirene was changed several times. During the Greek period it looked like an Ionian stoa. Later, there were 6 narrow entrances to the fountain. Pausanias writes, "The fountain is decorated with white marble, and hollow cavities have been hollowed out from which the water ran into the open. It is a water that is good to drink." It was considered the healthiest water in Greece. The architecture of the courtyard in front of the fountain was likewise varied according to the age: extremely simple during the Archaic Age, it was given a more impressive design by Herodes Atticus during the second century A. D. On three sides of the quadrangular courtyard there was a structure with an exedra, ornamented with marble and with niches for statues. In the centre was the fountain. During the Roman period, the Peirene Fountain was one of the most impressive monuments in Corinth.

It was discovered by archaeologists of the American School in 1898. There were three inscriptions which gave its exact location. In the third basin they found traces of a painting with fish, dating from Roman times.

The Fountain of Peirene was in use from earliest times down to the end of the 19th century. Today the Peirene Fountain supplies the village of Old-Corinth with water.

The Propylaea

The first-century Propylaea was the impressive main entrance to the Agora of Corinth from Lechaion Street. It was in marble and took the form of a triumphal arch with a large central thoroughfare (12 feet) and two smaller lateral passageways. According to Pausanias, it was surmounted by a gilt representation of Helius, the sun-god, and of Phaëthon, his son. Beside it was a statue of Heracles. Steps led from Lechaion Street to the Propylaea and to the Agora.

THE AGORA

The Agora at Corinth was one of the largest in Greece. A large space, which was 246 yards long from east to west and 140 yards wide, was paved with marble slabs and divided into two level terraces. The Agora of the Greek period, completely redesigned under the Romans in the year 146 A. D., was considerably smaller and paved with large pebblestones.

Pausanias has the following to say, "At the centre of the Agora is a statue of the goddess Athene, with reliefs of the Muses on its base".

As a matter of fact, the remains of a large altar and of numerous statues were uncovered at the centre of the Agora — perhaps one of them that of the goddess Athene.

Four main streets led off from the Agora. To the north, as we have seen, Lechaion Street; to the south, the road leading to Cenchreae, Corinth's harbour on the Saronic Gulf; to the north-west that leading to Sikyon; and to the west the road conducting to the Acrocorinth. During Roman times there was a large building with a very fine terraced staircase to the Agora. This building has been dubbed the Julian Basilica, because large portions of statues of members of Julius Caesar's family were found among the remains here.

West of this basilica the Roman surface has been excavated to expose that of the Greek Agora (approx. 40 inches lower). Here, too, the start for races with up to 16 runners was also found; it can still be seen today. This proves that during the Greek period there was also a stadium on the Agora. Starting from the southern corner of the basilica, a line of 30 central shops ran along the entire length of the Agora from east to west and separated the upper from the lower Agora. In the centre of this line of shops and almost opposite the Propylaea was the forum (bema), a large tribune from which the Roman Proconsul addressed the people (plate 8). It was from this tribune that the Apostle Paul also spoke to the Roman Proconsul Gallio to defend his own actions and Christianity. A small Christian church was later erected above the remains of the tribune.

South Stoa (plates 15—19)

The southern end of the Agora was almost entirely enclosed by the South Stoa, one of the most extensive edifices of ancient Greece. It had two storeys and was some 525 feet long and a little more than 80 feet wide. It was fronted by a colonnade of 71 Doric columns, behind which was a second row of 34 Ionian columns. Along its southern side and behind the colonnades were two lines of 33 shops, possibly taverns, since each of the premises in the front row had a small well, some 40 feet deep, connected via a conduit system to the Peirene Fountain. Along the terrace north of the Stoa stood some 100 statues. The first floor of the Stoa may have served as a large reception hall. The Stoa was built in the 4th century B. C. and alterations were carried out on it in the second. Shortly afterwards it was destroyed by Lucius Mummius.

It was rebuilt under Julius Caesar. The shops or taverns were replaced by a row of public buildings, the assembly hall for the competitors in the Isthmian Games and the office of the Roman Proconsul, where numerous mosaic floors were discovered (today roofed over). A large entrance led from the South Stoa to the South Basilica. This was very similar to the Julian Basilica and housed statues of the emperors. From the centre of the Stoa, the paved road led for 70 stadia (7.5 miles) to Cenchreae. The town hall (bouleuterion), a horse-shoe shaped edifice, lay to the west of this road, amidst the rows of shops already mentioned. There was another row of shops along the west side of the Agora. At a short distance from them, in the western section of the Agora, there were *six small Roman temples* standing almost in line. From south to north, we have the Temple of Fortuna (Temple F on the plan) and then Temple G, the pantheon, the sanctuary dedicated to the honour of all the gods. Pausanias relates that, not far from this latter temple, there was a fountain with a statue of Poseidon with a dolphin at his feet, a statue of Apollo, one of Aphrodite, two of Hermes and three of Zeus. Later two small temples, Temple H (perhaps dedicated to Heracles) and Temple J (possibly of Poseidon), were erected on the site of this fountain. Right next to them, there is a round monument to Babbius Philinus and two small temples, K and D, perhaps in honour of Hermes.

The Northern Side of the Agora

On the western side, next to the propylaea, there was the socalled "Façade of the Captives" (plate 14). This was a large two-storey building with its façade overlooking the Agora and graced with Corinthian columns. On the upper floor, there were instead of the four central columns four huge marble statues representing captive barbarians bearing the roof of the structure. Remains of these central statues are on view in the Museum.

Today, going off slantwise to the west of this façade, there is a wall with a 5th-century Doric frieze with triglyphs and metopes of coloured stone from Poros (Calauria). Here was the *Sacred Spring* (plate 13) which originally gushed forth in the open and was only roofed over later.

A stairway of seven steps led to this spring. The water ran out of two brazen lion-heads which can still be seen in the wall opposite the stairway. Near the Sacred Spring and connected with it there was a small oracle shrine (marked B on the plan). The water of the Sacred Spring was used for religious purposes.

On the north-west side of the Agora, there was another line of shops. In the middle of these 15 Roman shops (1st century A. D.) one still has its vaulting intact. It is the most impressive of the surviving buildings in the Agora (plates 7 and 13).

Behind the shops was the North-West Stoa of the Hellenistic Period (3rd century), consisting of an outer row of Doric columns and an inner line of Corinthian.

To the north of the Stoa and on a slight elevation stood the Temple of Apollo.

THE TEMPLE OF APOLLO (plates 3—5 and 12, 20, 22)

The Temple of Apollo is situated to the north-west of the Agora on a terrace. It dominates the entire archaeological zone, the Agora and the surrounding area. From it the visitor is granted a magnificent view extending as far as the waters of the Corinthian Gulf.

The Temple of Apollo is one of the most ancient and most important among the surviving temples on the Greek mainland. It was erected in the years 550—525 B. C. to replace a 7th-century temple. The Temple of Apollo was a Doric peripteros with 6 columns at both ends and 15 along each side (38 in all). It was 174 feet long and almost 70 feet wide. The monolithic Doric columns of poros stone have severe archaic capitals and 23 flutes. They were over 23 feet high and had a diameter of 5 feet 8 inches at the base. 7 of them are still standing: five at the west end and 2 on the south side. The architrave still tops 5 of the columns in the south-west corner.

A piece of the cyma is among the exhibits in the Museum. The Temple consisted of a pronaos with two columns in antis, a three-aisled cella with rows of four columns (bearing the roof), an adyton with 4 columns and an opisthodomos to the west again with two columns in antis.

According to Pausanias there was a brazen statue of Apollo in the Temple. In Greek times there was a large stairway to the east of the temple area which led down to Lechaion street and to the entrance to the Agora.

This Temple with its few surviving columns was all that was visible before the excavations began and the only indication of possible finds to be made here. To the north of the Temple, there was a North Market, at a somewhat lower level; today it is partially covered by other buildings. At the north-west corner of the Agora, the road leading to Sikyon began. It ran along the west of the Temple of Apollo. To the left of this road there is a temple (C on the plan) which was perhaps the sanctuary and temple of Hera Akraia.

Temple E (plate 21) is a large Roman temple of the 1st century A. D., possibly of Octavia, the sister of the Emperor Augustus. Such a temple is mentioned by Pausanias (II, 3, 1).

THE MUSEUM

The Museum's exhibits are all finds from the excavations made in the Agora at Corinth and from the regions around Corinth. There are three exhibition rooms. On the left of the small first room we enter, we see the prehistoric finds from the neolithic and later periods (plates 23—27). In the second room to the right of the entrance there are remarkable examples of Greek ceramic art from the Archaic to Classical times. Corinthian ceramic ware of the 7th and 6th centuries was famous and was also exported (plates 28—41). The font for sacred water, which once stood in the museum at Corinth, was transferred to this new museum on the Isthmus, where indeed it rightly belongs. The third room, to the left of the entrance, contains statues and mosaics mainly of Roman times as well as numerous Roman copies of classical statues (plates 44—52). Here, too, are the 7 Roman statues of emperors that were found in the "Basilica Julia". Against the far wall are the huge statues of captives from the "Captives' Façade" in the Agora and a sarcophagus with a relief of the departure of the "Seven Against Thebes" and of Opheltes dying from the serpent's bite (plates 48, 50).

The Fountain of Glauke (plates 53, 55)

When we leave the enclosed zone, we see on our right a large cubic rock with four big basins for a fountain, just like the Peirene Fountain. As Pausanias (II, 3, 6) informs us, the fountain draws its name from the daughter of Creon, the king of Corinth, who became Jason's second wife. When Medea, his first wife, heard of the wedding, she sent Glauke (or Creusa) a magic robe as a wedding gown. As soon as Glauke donned the new robe, it burst into flames; in an attempt to assuage the terrible pains she suffered, she threw herself into the waters of the fountain which now bears her name.

OUTSIDE THE ARCHAEOLOGICAL ZONE

Odeion (plate 54)

Outside and to the north-west of the archaeological zone we see the remains of the Odeion (Odeum). The Odeion, which is in part hewn out of the rock, was built towards the end of the 1st century A. D. and seated 3000. It was restored by Herodes Atticus in 170—175 A. D. At that time the northern peristyle was built (cf. plan), which linked Odeion and Theatre to form one complex. It was destroyed by fire in the 3rd century and was then transformed into an arena for contests with wild animals and gladiatorial shows. The Odeion was finally destroyed once and for all towards the end of the 4th century.

Theatre (plate 56)

The Theatre was built in the 5th century B. C. and could seat 18,000. It was completely restored under the Romans and was likewise converted into an arena in which nautical events were staged. The seats of the Greek period are better preserved because they were covered with earth before the new seats were erected over them.
On the wall of the orchestra the excavations have revealed painted representations of contests with wild animals and between gladiators. An inscription was also found which tells the story of Androcles and the Lion.

THE ACROCORINTH (plates 57—59)

A tour of Corinth would not be complete without a visit to the Acrocorinth. The visitor is repaid for the ascent with a splendid view of the Saronic and Corinthian Gulfs and also of the plain of Corinth. The hill is about 1885 feet high and bears traces of all the periods of its history. The main entrance is protected by a triple defensive wall. In addition to a small temple of the Warlike Aphrodite, there is also a subterranean cistern. This was known as the "Upper Peirene", since it was believed in antiquity that the waters of the "Lower Peirene" were fed from here. Everywhere on the Acrocorinth there are ruins from various periods which bear witness to a past as eventful as that of Old-Corinth.

✳

1   Sima and gutter from the Temple of Apollo
     Cimaise et gouttière du Temple d'Apollon
     Wasserspeier vom Dach des Apollo-Tempels

KORINTHOS

CORINTH   CORINTHE   KORINTH

2   Lechaion Road and the Acrocorinth   Rue de Léchaion et l'Acrocorinthe   Lechaionstraße und Akrokorinth

Le Temple d'Apollon   Der Tempel des Apollo

5 Part of the Agora and the Temple of Apollo
   L'Agora et le Temple d'Apollon
   Teil der Agora und der Apollotempel

6 Large stairway leading to the Temple
   Grand escalier menant à la terrasse du Temple
   Große Treppe, die zum Tempel führt

7 Agora. Northwest shops
   Les boutiques du côté nord-ouest de l'Agora
   Geschäfte an der Nordwestseite der Agora

8   Bema and Acrocorinth
     Bêma et Acrocorinthe
     Bema (Rednertribüne) und Akrokorinth

9   Starting line in the Stadium of the Greek Agora
     Ligne de départ au Stade de l'Agora grecque
     Startschwellen im Stadion der griechischen Agora

10   Pavement of the Greek Agora
     Pavement de l'Agora grecque
     Boden der griechischen Agora

(Memoria:
Paulus ad
Corinthios)

11   Fountain of Peirene
     Fontaine Pirène
     Peirene-Quelle

12
The Temple
Le Temple
Der Tempel

13   Agora and Sacred Spring   L'Agora et la Fontaine sacrée   Agora und Heilige Quelle

14   Captives Façade   Façade des Barbares captifs   Sog. „Fassade der Gefangenen"

15 16 17 South Stoa La Stoa du sud Südliche Stoa

18 19 Southern shops and paved road to Kenchreai
        Boutiques du sud et route pavée menant à Kenchréai
        Südliche Reihe von Geschäften und der Weg nach Kenchreä

20 Apollo Temple
    Le Temple d'Apollon ▷ ▷
    Der Apollotempel

21   Roman Temple E   Temple Romain E   Römischer Tempel E

22 Apollo Temple   Le Temple d'Apollon   Der Tempel des Apollo

23 24   3000 a. C.
Early Neolithic Vases
Vases du Néolithique Ancien
Gefäße aus der Frühneolithischen Zeit

25 26 27
Mycenaean Vases
Vases Mycéniens
Mykenische Vasen
1500—1200 a. C.

28
Geometric Vase
Vase de style géo-
métrique
Geometrische Vase
VIII. s. a. C.

29
Figurine from Potters'
Quarter
Figurine en terre cuite
Kleine Terrakotta-Figur
650 a. C.

33   Corinthian Vase   Vase Corinthien   Korinthisches Gefäß   625–550 a. C.

30   Corinthian Cylix   Cylix Corinthienne   Korinthische Kylix   625–600 a. C.

31 32   Corinthian Vases   Vases Corinthiens   Korinthische Gefäße   625–600 a. C.

35   Corinthian Vase
Vase Corinthien
Korinthische Kanne
625–600 a. C.

36 37 Corinthian Vases
Vases Corinthiens
Korinthische Gefäße
625–600 a. C.

38 39   Attic black-figured Cylix   Cylix Attique à figures noires   Attische schwarzfigurige Kylix   550—500 a. C.

40 41 Attic black-figured Cylix Cylix Attique à figures noires Attische schwarzfigurige Kylix 550—500 a. C.

42   Head of a Kouros   Tête d'un Kouros archaïque   Kopf eines archaischen Kuros   1. Qu. V. s. a. C.

43   Female head   Hellenistic period   Tête feminine   Weiblicher Kopf

44   Head of Serapis   Tête de Sérapis   Kopf des Serapis

45   Head of Fortuna (Tyche)   End of first cent.   Tête de Tyché (Fortune)   Kopf der Tyche (Fortuna)

49   Head of Dionysos   Tête de Dionysos   Kopf des Dionysos

46   Doryphoros of Polykleitos. Roman copy   Le Doryphore de Polyclète   Der Doryphoros des Polykleitos
47   Head of Nero, son of Germanicus   Tête de Néron, fils de Germanicus   Kopf des Nero, Sohn des Germanicus
48   Captive barbarian from the '' Captives' Façade '' in the Agora — Statue de la « Façade des Captifs
Barbares » sur l'Agora — Kriegsgefangener von der „Fassade der Gefangenen" in der Agora

53 The Fountain of Glauke   La Fontaine de Glauké   Die Quelle der Glauke
54 The Roman Odeion   L'Odéon Romain   Das Römische Odeon

55   The Fountain of Glauke   La Fontaine de Glauké   Die Quelle der Glauke

56   The ancient Theatre   Les ruines du Théâtre   Die Ruinen des Theaters

57

The Temple of Aphrodite
Le Temple d'Aphrodite
Der Tempel der Aphrodite

58

Gate and Fortifications
Les murs de la forteresse
Die Mauern der Festung

MYCENAE

FROM OLD-CORINTH TO MYCENAE VIA NEMEA

To visit Mycenae from Corinth, one follows the main road leading south to Argos and Tripolis. A road that turns off to the right just past the railway station conducts the visitor to the "sacred precincts" of ancient *Nemea,* today the village of Iraklio (Heracleion, a little more than 3 miles from the railway station). Here a Doric temple dedicated to the Nemean Zeus was built in the 4th century B. C. It was constructed in tufa above the ruins of an older temple. Today only three columns survive. The area around this temple was sacred and here it was that first the inhabitants of Cleonae and later the Argives as well staged games: *the Nemean Games.* They were held in honour of Heracles who, the saga tells us, slew the lion which terrorized the region. This explains why Heracles is shown on all reliefs and vases with the lion on his shoulder as a symbol of strength. Another explanation has also come down to us: under their leader Adrastus the "Seven" set out with their armies against Thebes. In the vicinity of Nemea they were afflicted by great thirst. They met Hypsipyle, the nurse of Opheltes, son of King Lycurgus, and bade her to show them a spring. She did so, leaving the young Opheltes on his own, although an oracle had warned that he was not to be left alone before he could walk. While she was gone, the serpent that watched over the spring bit Opheltes, a bite which proved fatal. The "Seven" interpreted this as a bad omen, interrupted their march and organized games lasting three days in honour of Opheltes.

The Nemean Games were held every two years and the victors were crowned with a wreath of wild celery. From the year 573 B. C. the Games assumed a pan-Hellenic character.

After this short visit to Nemea, we return to the main road and continue on our way to Argos. In so doing, we drive through the important *Pass of Dervenakia.* Here in 1822 Theodoros Kolokotrones, the leader of the rebellious Greeks on the Peloponnesus, annihilated the Turkish army of Dramali, who had marched into the Peloponnesus to put down the revolt of the Greeks there.

Afterwards, we come to the village of Phichtia, where we turn off left to arrive after some 2 1/2 miles at the famous archaeological site of Mycenae. Our first impression here is rather disappointing.

To the east we see the *Acropolis of Mycenae* on the summit of a rocky hill. It is enclosed by Cyclopean walls and within and without there is nothing but ruins and destruction. To the north and south we see two bare hills, Prophet Élias and Sara, which brood like two great rocky guards over the Acropolis. Nowhere is there any vegetation: there are no trees to offer the visitor shade from the summer heat or to break the monotony of the desolate rocky landscape. One naturally asks oneself why the original inhabitants of Mycenae chose this of all sites to dwell in. However, as soon as one has climbed up on to the Acropolis, one is rewarded with a view of a farspread and colourful landscape: a plain stretching from Dervenakia to the bay of Argos and generously endowed with lemon, mandarine, orange, peach and apricot trees.

It was this hill, a natural fortress and a first-rate observation post for the whole of the Argolic Plain, which was selected by the inhabitants of Mycenae for their township. Their kings had it fortified with Cyclopean walls and erected their palaces here.

LEGENDS ASSOCIATED WITH PERSEUS

The life of Perseus was filled with adventure. Even before he was born, King Acrisius was informed by an oracle that he would be killed by his daughter's son. Thus he imprisoned his daughter Danaë in a bronze underground chamber as soon as she reached marriageable age. However, Zeus, who had fallen in love with Danaë, transformed himself into a shower of golden rain and so got to her. The child of this embrace was Perseus. Now, in order to ensure that the oracle should not be fulfilled, Acrisius shut his daughter and grandson in a chest and cast them into the sea. Waves carried the chest safely to the island of Seriphus. There they were found by Dictys, the brother of the king. He brought Danaë and Perseus to Polydectes, his brother, who was then king of the island. When Perseus had grown to manhood, Polydectes sent him to get the head of the Gorgon Medusa. Her face turned whoever looked upon it into stone and instead of hair she had writhing serpents. With the aid of the goddess Athena and the god Hermes, he was able to carry out this task. Afterwards in Ethiopia he rescued Andromeda, the King's daughter, from a sea monster. He married her and returned with her to Seriphus, taking the head of the Medusa with him. When Polydectes' eyes fell on this, he was turned to stone. Perseus then gave the head of the Medusa to his protectress, Athena, who from then on always bore it on her aegis.

Together with his mother, Danaë, and his wife, Andromeda, Perseus now returned to Argos only to find that Acrisius, his grandfather, was away in Larissa in Thessaly. Perseus decided also to go there to take part in the funeral games. When he threw the discus, he accidentally hit and killed his grandfather, who was among the spectators. Perseus was so affected by his death that, when he arrived back at Argos, he handed over the sovereignty there to his cousin, Megapenthes, and himself assumed the kingship of Tiryns and founded Midea and Mycenae.

After the death of Perseus, who tradition tells us was the founder of Mycenae, his offspring were on the throne for three generations: Elektryon, Sthenelus and Eurystheus. During the reign of Sthenelus, the twin brothers Thyestes and Atreus were banished from Olympia by their father, Pelops, for killing their half-brother Chrysippus. They both fled to Mycenae, since Sthenelus was married to their sister, Nicippe. On Sthenelus'death, he was succeeded by his son, Eurystheus, as King of Mycenae. It was he who imposed the 12 labours on Heracles and it was he who banished the Heraclidae, after the death of Heracles, and forced them to leave the Peloponnesus and flee to Attica.

Since the Athenians offered them refuge and gave them land to settle on, Eurystheus determined on a punitory expedition against Athens. In the ensuing battle, the Mycenaeans were slain by Heracles' sons.

During his absence, Eurystheus had left Atreus behind as his representative. On the death of Eurystheus and his sons, the Mycenaeans made Atreus their king. This marked the end of the line of Perseus and the beginning of the house of Atreus on the Mycenaean throne. According to the legendary early history of Mycenae, an implacable hatred arose between Atreus and his brother when the former ascended the throne.

THE HOUSE OF ATREUS

The house of Atreus is characterized by frightful antitheses. On the one hand, the Mycenaean culture flourished and advanced in all branches of human endeavour; on the other, monstrous crimes that almost evade human understanding were committed. From Tantalus, the father of Pelops, to Orestes, the son of Agamemnon and Clytemnestra, so many deeds of madness afflict the line of Pelops that one might think a divine curse had fallen on it: a goldmine for the Greek tragedians of genius. The throne passed from Atreus to Thyestes and from Thyestes to Agamemnon, the best-known king of Mycenae, for it was during his reign that the Greeks laid siege to Troy. Agamemnon was the commander-in-chief of all the Greek forces. He was at the head of this mighty army and had a hundred ships under him. In the Iliad, Homer calls Agamemnon the king of kings. During the reign of Agamemnon, Mycenae was in possession of so much gold that Homer dubs it "golden" Mycenae.

The house of Atreus lived and reigned during the period when the Mycenaean culture was at its zenith. After the destruction of Troy, Agamemnon returned to Mycenae as the victor laden with trophies.

Awaiting him was an inglorious death. His own wife, Clytemnestra, murdered him, aided and abetted by her lover, Aegisthus. Eight years later, when Orestes had grown to manhood, he revenged his father's death by killing both his mother, Clytemnestra, and her paramour, Aegisthus. After the murder of his mother, Orestes was pursued by the Erinyes (Furies) and wandered from town to town in Greece. But nowhere did he find relief. He then sought counsel in Delphi and Apollo advised him to go to Athens and place himself at the mercy of Athena. Athena summoned the Areopagus to try him. Apollo himself was his advocate and, when the jury reached a tie, Athena cast her deciding vote in Orestes' favour. Thus, Orestes was able to return to Mycenae, where he became king about the year 1100 B. C.

The Mycenaean culture had begun to develop and come to fruition long before the year 1400 B. C. in fact. However, 1400—1200 were the years when Mycenae enjoyed the greatest prosperity in trade and shipping and art. A terrible earthquake which was caused by a volcanic eruption on the island of Thera (Santorin) around 1450 B. C. and which submerged about half the island also wreaked terrible havoc among the Minoan towns along the north coast of Crete and thus enabled Mycenae to expand its activities. Competition arose between Mycenae and Crete with the result that Crete was slowy but surely edged out of the Aegean and Mycenae was able to assume the dominant role not only in the Aegean and in the Ionian Sea, but throughout the entire eastern Mediterranean as well.

Like all peoples and civilizations that experience a period of prosperity followed by inevitable decline, Mycenae too started to decline after it had attained to such power, wealth and fame. The Trojan War had so weakened the Greeks who had taken part in it that the Dorians, another traditional branch of the ancient Greek people, invading the Peloponnesus from Thessaly, were easily able to conquer the Achaeans. Mycenae was razed. All the Achaeans that could fled to Aegialia or to Crete; those that remained were enslaved by the new lords.

The Dorian invasion marks the end of Mycenaean supremacy. From a powerful city-state it was reduced to a town of no importance. And so it remained until the time of the Persian Wars. On the memory of the Greeks, Mycenae and the royal line of Atreus are imprinted not as an historical reality but rather as a legend. In classical times, under the influence of Tradition and Homer, the tragic dramatists Aeschylus, Sophocles and Euripides so immortalized Atreus and his descendants that they are better known to us than Mycenae itself.

Pausanias related that the Argives destroyed Mycenae out of petty jealousy, because they had remained neutral during the invasion of the Medes, whereas the Mycenaeans had sent a contingent of 80 to join in the stand at Thermopylae where all fell to a man at the side of the Spartans (Herodotus VII, 202).

In the following year of 479 B. C., 400 Mycenaeans as well as inhabitants of Tiryns took part in the Battle of Plataea against the Persians. The Spartan stand at Thermopylae brought them great glory which also reflected on the Mycenaeans. And the cities which had taken part in the great victory at the Battle of Plataea also enjoyed a similar renown. From the rich booty won at Plataea, the Greeks dedicated a votive offering to Apollo: it was a gold tripod of three snakes whose bodies were entwined and whose heads supported the basin. The names of those towns that had taken part in the Battle of Plataea, among them also that of Mycenae, were engraved on the curving bodies of the snakes. This twofold fame aroused the enmity and envy of the Argives who laid siege to Mycenae around the year 460 B. C. and completely razed it after they had taken it. Tiryns suffered the same fate.

200 years later, during the Hellenistic era, c. 268, the Argives repaired the damage they had done to the Cyclopean walls and resettled the Acropolis at the top of the hill and also the area down below.

At this time, too, it may be presumed that a temple dedicated to the goddess Athena was erected on the summit of the hill on the foundations of an Archaic temple of the 7th century B. C. The excavations have uncovered traces of both these temples. Pausanias tells us (II 16, 3—7) that, when he visited Mycenae in the second century B. C., he saw the Cyclopean Walls, the Lion Gate, works of the Cyclopes, the Fountain of Perseia and the subterranean structures of Atreus and his sons where they stored their treasures. He also mentions graves of Atreus, of Agamemnon, of Eurymedon, Agamemnon's charioteer, and of Electra. Clytemnestra and Aegisthus were buried just outside the walls, since they were not deemed worthy to be interred within them where the graves of Agamemnon and all those who were slain with him were located.

Pausanias also adds that Perseus named this site Mycenae because on this spot his "mykes" (scabbard) fell to the ground or because it was here that he was so overcome by thirst that he plucked a "myketa" (mushroom) and finding drinking-water interpreted this as a good sign.

Pausanias does not indicate whether the site was inhabited or not when he visited it. After Pausanias, who is also the last classical writer to write about Mycenae, the town fell into oblivion. It is not mentioned again until the days of Turkish domination in the 18th and 19th centuries, and then not as a town but as an unguarded site where finding was keeping.

Among the foreigners who removed relics of antiquity were once again Lord Elgin and Lord Sligo and Veli Pasha of Nauplion.

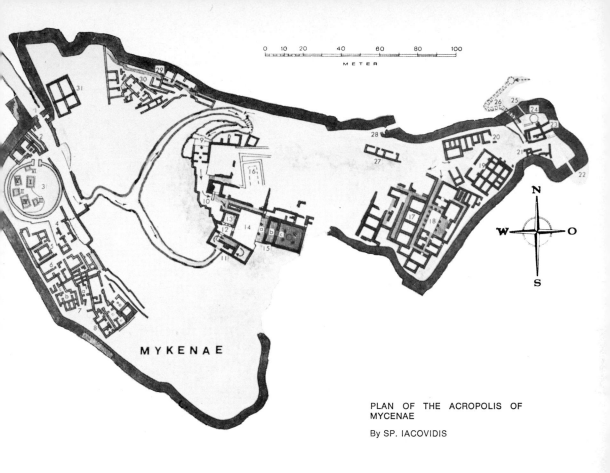

MYKENAE

PLAN OF THE ACROPOLIS OF MYCENAE

By SP. IACOVIDIS

1 The Lion Gate 2 Granary 3 Grave Circle A 4 Ramp House 5 House of the Warrior Vase 6 South House 7 House with the Idols 8 Tsountas' House 9 Propylon of the Palace 10 Entrance to the Palace 11 Great Staircase 12 Anteroom 13 Throne Room or Guestroom 14 Great Court 15 Megaron 16 Hellenistic Temple of Athena 17 The Artists' House 18 House of Columns 19, 20, 21 23, 27 Northeast Foundations 22, 25 Sally Port 24 Hellenistic Cistern 26 Secret Cistern 28 North Postern Gate 29 North Gallery 30, 31 Military Barracks

THE EXCAVATIONS

The Archaeological Society first undertook excavation work here in 1840 and laid bare the external court of the Lion Gate. However, it was Heinrich Schliemann who aroused the astonished admiration of the entire archaeological, scholarly and artistic world when he excavated here. Schliemann was not an archaeologist but an admirer of Homer and of all the writers of ancient Greece. He was utterly convinced that Homer's accounts were not mere fairy tales but that they reflected the reality of his day. It was with this belief and with his remarkable knack in developing his plans that he came to Greece to put his convictions to the test. Fate looked kindly on him: in 14 weeks Schliemann laid bare a hidden and forgotten treasure that had slumbered through the oblivion of centuries. The glittering treasures of reality were wrested from the darkness of forgetfulness: the world

21

was dazzled by the brightness of the gold unearthed from the graves. It was the dawn of a new epoch for the science of archaeology and for the history of art. An unknown culture was exposed to the glare of publicity. The boundaries of history, till then so narrow, suddenly took on new dimensions. Prehistory became history; a glimpse was had of the kernel of truth behind the sagas and legends.

The 5 royal graves that Schliemann excavated and the sixth unearthed by Stamatakis make up the royal Grave Circle A.

After Schliemann, Christos Tsoundas spent 18 years in studying and excavating Mycenae. During this time, he discovered the palace on the summit of the hill, the subterranean cistern and a number of beehive graves outside the Acropolis. This scholarly and archaeological investigation was continued by Alan J. B. Wace, with interruptions, from 1919 to 1957. Wace's painstaking and exact studies completed the work of Schliemann and Tsoundas and fixed the chronology of the beehive graves and cast light on the funerary customs of the inhabitants of Mycenae. He also studied the structures outside the Acropolis. While attempting to restore the collapsed roof of the grave of Clytemnestra in the year 1951, Joannis Papadimitriou discovered quite by chance Grave Circle B with its 24 graves. This Grave Circle yielded very valuable finds from the end of the 17th and the beginning of the 16th century B. C.

Since the death of Papadimitriou, Professor G. Mylonas has continued with the work of excavation and research at Mycenae.

ACROPOLIS: WALLS, LION GATE

The Acropolis was built in the north-eastern corner of the Argolic Plain on a natural rock triangular in shape and just over 900 feet high. To the south, the steep ravine Chavus separates the Acropolis from Mount Sara (approx. 1770 feet) and renders it impregnable from that side. To the north, the mountain known as Prophet Elias (approx. 2790 feet) rises up above the valley of Kokoretsa. The hill is enclosed on all sides by Cyclopean walls. These walls, like those at Tiryns, are the most impressive and best preserved fortifications dating from the early period of Greek history. They are nearly 40 feet high and have an average thickness of 16 to 20 feet. They are constructed of huge unhewn stones which were laid lengthwise one upon the other; the intervening spaces were filled with smaller stones and clay.

Legend tells us that the Cyclopes learnt the art of building from Hephaestus, the smith-god, himself. When later Perseus became king of Mycenae he had the fortifications of the Acropolis built by the Cyclopes.

The Acropolis was constructed in three stages: first the gate looked south and walls were so built that Grave Circle A was outside them. In the second phase (c. 1250 B. C.) the walls were moved further south so as to enclose the graves just mentioned. At this time the powerful Lion Gate looking north was constructed.

For the new Cyclopean walls east of the Lion Gate, hewn stones were employed which fitted each other exactly. The tower on the west wall was built with the same type of stone so that the entrance seen as a whole was imparted a stately dignity. They also erected the gate in the north wall.

It was probably not until the 3rd century B. C. that the polygonal section of the wall system that we find on the external side of the wall south-west of the Lion Gate and another southern section were built.

The External Court (plate 62)

In front of the Lion Gate the walls rising up on the east and west sides form a narrow court, some 40 feet long and 24 feet wide. This rendered a massed assault on the citadel impossible.

The Lion Gate (plates 61—63)

The main entrance to the Acropolis of Mycenae is the Lion Gate. This mighty and dignified structure impressively mirrors two epochs: the mythical and the historical, and tells of the power of the line of Atreus.

The Gate is roughly square in shape and a little over 10 feet in height. At the bottom it is 9 feet 8 inches wide; it narrows towards the top. The Gate was constructed of four hewn stones: the base is one great stone 15 feet 3 inches long, 7 feet 7 inches wide and 2 feet 10 inches high.

The stones employed for the actual Gate are also monoliths: they are a little over 10 feet high, 5 feet 8 inches long and just under 2 feet wide. It is these two lateral gate posts that support the ends of the enormous block of stone forming the upper part of the Gate: it is estimated to weigh 18 tonnes. It is 14 feet 9 inches long, 6 feet 6 inches wide and of an average thickness of 2 feet 7 inches. There is a relieving triangle over the lintel which serves to distribute the main weight of the gate on to the vertical posts of the gate. It is filled with a triangular slab of limestone on which two lions are represented: the slab is almost 11 feet high, close to 3 feet thick and 12 feet 9 inches at its base. The two lions are shown in profile and confronting each other; their rear paws almost touch the upper portion of the gate and their front paws rest on slabs which combine to form two altars; on these stands a Minoan column between the two lions. Their heads have not survived; presumably they were turned in the direction of new arrivals. Originally two wooden doorleaves secured the gateway.

GRAVE CIRCLE A (plates 64, 66, 69)

On passing through the gateway and coming to a halt in the small interior, one sees to the right the foundations of structures which were connected with the Cyclopean walls. These have been seen as a granary on account of the charred grain found in jugs there. However, they can just as easily have formed a guardroom.

Still, what particularly arouses the interest of visitors is the Grave Circle A that formed a particularly sacred area. Schliemann excavated this in the year 1876.

Two rows of vertical slabs arranged in circles enclosed the graves. The empty space between the two rows (4 feet 5 inches) was filled with earth and covered with horizontal slabs. This gave a certain regularity of appearance to the circle, which was a little more than 91 feet in diameter. The entrance on the northern side was constructed of the same stone. It was here that 6 royal shaft graves with rich funerary gifts artistically worked in gold were found. When Schliemann excavated his five royal graves, he followed the description of Pausanias according to which there were the 5 tombs of Agamemnon and his followers in Mycenae. He stopped when he had found them; his thirst for knowledge had been quenched and he went away satisfied. Accordingly, he named the gold mask which is now in the National Museum at Athens the mask of Agamemnon (plate 89). Stamatakis, a member of the Archaeological Society, continued with the digs, and it was he who found the sixth grave. In the same area, but actually outside the Grave Circle, Drosinos, Schliemann's engineer, found in an old shaft a treasure of rich funerary gifts belonging to one of the royal graves.

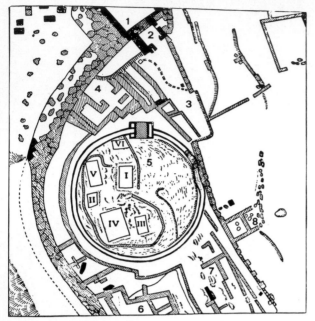

PLAN OF THE GRAVE CIRCLE A
1 The Lion Gate 2 Inside the Gate 3 The Ramp 4 The Granary 5 Grave Circle A I—VI The Royal Graves 6 House of the Warrior Vase 7 Ramp House 8 Hellenistic Chambers

In the year 1956, Papadimitriou uncovered a fairly shallow grave with the skeleton of a man and two earthenware vessels. There had accordingly been other graves that had been too insignificant to merit greater respect.

The royal graves of Circle A were shaft graves and of various sizes: the largest measured roughly 15 x 21 feet, the smallest some 10 x 11½ feet. The funerary gifts witness to such an abundance of gold and such exquisite artistry that not only did they impress Schliemann and the scholars of his day but they still do not fail to produce their effect on the present-day beholder. This entire Mycenaean treasure, of which alone the gold weighs 14 kilos (31 lbs), is now on view in the Mycenaean Hall of the National Museum at Athens (plates 65, 76—86 and 89—92).

When the graves were dug, small walls, 2½ to 5 feet high and a little more than 1 foot thick, rose at the sides. Alongside the dead, who were buried fully clothed, gifts were placed which it was felt the deceased would need on his journey through Hades.

Wooden posts were laid close together on the little walls and then covered with slabs or with reeds and dried herbs and finally with a layer of clay. Any remaining spaces were then filled with earth up to the surface. Here the relatives and friends of the dead sat for the funeral repast. When they had completed the meal, they covered the whole with earth to form a grave mound on which they then placed the funerary stele. 19 skeletons, 8 of males, 9 of females and 2 of children, were found in the royal graves of Circle A.

Following the research and the first enthusiastic publications made by Schliemann, the scholars who studied the funerary gifts of the royal graves more closely proved that the shaft graves of Circle A are of still greater antiquity than the era of Agamemnon and in fact date from the 16th century (approx. 1600—1510 B. C.). Since Agamemnon lived around 1225—1180 B. C., it is quite clear that they could not date from his age. They must therefore go back to a dynasty of unknown kings who reigned in Mycenae in those prehistoric times, i. e. in the 16th century B. C. Neither can they stem from Perseus and his successors, since Perseus, to whom the foundation of the city is ascribed, reigned in Mycenae c. 1400—1350 B. C.

Outside and to the south of Grave Circle A, the foundation walls of 5 edifices have

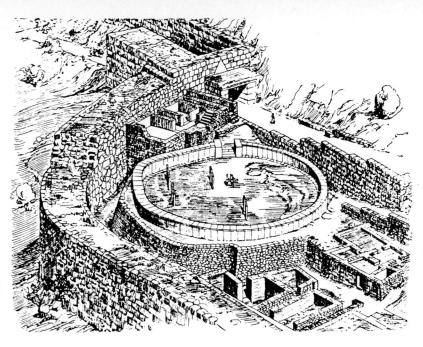

Reconstruction of Grave Circle A with the Cyclopean Walls. (By Alan Wace)

survived. These have been named either after the archaeologists who excavated them or after the finds made in them.

1) House of the Warrior Vase

In the ruins of this building Schliemann found pieces of a large vase decorated with the representation of Mycenaean warriors. Today the vase is to be seen in the National Museum (plate 65). During later excavations, 16 Middle Helladic graves were also uncovered.

2) House beneath the steep ramp leading to the Palace

This ramp house had two storeys and a large hall. Here the famous treasure mentioned above was found.

3) South House

This is situated to the south of the House of the Warrior Vase. Here ten vessels were dug up.

4) House of the Idols or Wace's House

During the last excavations, a sanctuary with a central hearth and a series of benches and steps were laid bare. On one of them a statuette of terracotta and in front of it a small table for offerings were found. A step led to another small room in which there were sacred images, terracotta snakes, jewelry and votive offerings.

West of this sanctuary, the excavations uncovered another large room with a central hearth and a mural of a religious scene in which women were taking part (the mural and the other finds can all be viewed in the Museum at Nauplion).

5) Tsounta's House

This house was situated to the south-east of the last named and was excavated by Tsounta in 1886. Further excavations were carried out there in 1950, 1959 and 1960. In view of the steepness of the site, the house had three storeys: the second housed a hall, the third a sanctuary.

THE PALACE RAMP (plate 66 left)

Not far from, but to the east of, Grave Circle A there is a Cyclopean wall which supports the steep ramp leading from the Lion Gate to the Palace. It was 19 to 20 feet wide and ran parallel to the wall.
Originally it curved round to the north and led to the great staircase to the Palace. This wide roadway was used for the royal carriages passing to and from the Palace.
Today only a small section at the beginning, some 80 feet in length, has survived; it is broken by the foundation wall of an Hellenistic structure, perhaps an olive press. Today the ascent to the palace is via a steep path that leads straight to the north-west entrance.

THE PALACE

At the height of its prosperity the Palace erected on the summit of the Acropolis enclosed according to the calculations of experts an area of roughly 250 × 425 feet. The irreparable damage that has been wrought on the complex renders a reconstruction impossible, even for the most gifted of imaginations.
What has survived are essentially the foundation walls of the south-western side where the Megaron is also situated. The Palace had two entrances: one on the north-west and the second on the south-west side. Here, too, was the Great Staircase (plate 68).
In Wace's view this latter was the main entrance to the Palace. However, Professor G. Mylonas is of the opinion that this was probably the north-west entrance, where in fact we will begin our description of the Palace.
The visitor arrives via the steep path directly at the north-west foregate in front of which was a court. On the northern, external side of the Palace and near to this court there were two rooms for the guards of the gate. Farther to the north-east we see stone steps of the northern staircase. This foregate was quadrangular in shape and there was one column standing in both the inner and the outer hall.
Adjacent to the inner hall is a court from which we arrive via the west corridor at the Palace entrance, of which only the lower section has survived. Of the two galleries the northern (left) led to the royal apartments and the southern to the Great Court.

GREAT COURT (plate 70)

The Great Court — approximately 50 feet long and 40 feet wide — was not roofed over. It would appear that the Palace had a second storey, so that some of the windows would have overlooked the Court. The floor was finished in mortar and then subdivided with red lines into a pattern of squares. The squares were red, yellow and blue in succession and ornamented with graphic symbols. A Mycenaean frieze of half-rosettes and triglyphs ran round the lower portion of the wall.
The Megaron, the most important and impressive room in the Palace, was situated to the east of the Great Court. It consisted of a Porch, a Vestibule and the actual Megaron itself. Along the Court side the Porch had two wooden pillars of which the foundations can still be seen. A double-wing door at the northern end of the Porch led to the royal chambers. A wide doorway, the lower section of which measured roughly 8 x 4 feet, gave access to the Vestibule to the east. The floor around the walls was of sandstone and the central section consisted of large squares painted with graphic symbols in blue, yellow and red.

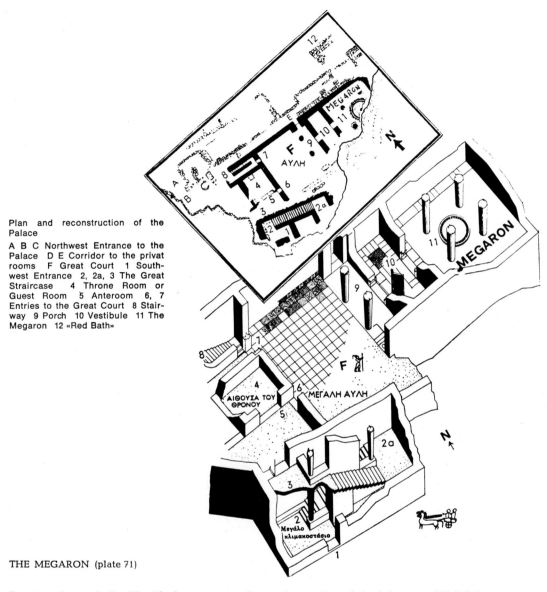

Plan and reconstruction of the Palace

A B C Northwest Entrance to the Palace D E Corridor to the privat rooms F Great Court 1 Southwest Entrance 2, 2a, 3 The Great Straircase 4 Throne Room or Guest Room 5 Anteroom 6, 7 Entries to the Great Court 8 Stairway 9 Porch 10 Vestibule 11 The Megaron 12 «Red Bath»

THE MEGARON (plate 71)

Passing through the Vestibule, we enter the main section of the Megaron (37 ft 9 in × 42 ft 8 in) which quite possibly was divided off from the Vestibule by a curtain and not a door. The floor was as in the Vestibule: around the edges in limestone and the rest in large painted squares. The walls were covered with murals and ornamented with the usual Mycenaean frieze (half-rosettes and triglyphs) around the lower section.

At the centre of the Megaron there was a circular hearth a little more than 11 feet in diameter and some 6 inches high and enclosed by a ring of fire-resistant flint. There were four wooden pillars arranged symmetrically around the hearth to support the high roof, which had a central opening to provide an outlet for the smoke.

The southern section of the Megaron collapsed into the Chavus ravine, taking nearly half of the structure with it and one of the pillar foundations. The reconstruction of this part by the Greek Office of Monument Conservation and Restoration gives an impression of what the Megaron must have looked like originally. The throne probably stood at the centre of the south wall — at the right of the entrance — as in the megara at Tiryns and Pylos. Perhaps there were also windows in the east wall providing a view of the Chavus ravine and the Argolic Plain.

A door pierced the west wall of the Great Hall and led to a Vestibule which was not roofed over. To the north and adjacent to it, there was a room (18 x 20 feet) which Wace identified as the Throne Room, whereas G. Mylonas regards it as a Guest Room because in his view the Megaron also served as the Throne Room. The Palace visitor reached this Vestibule by ascending the Great Staircase already mentioned. Some 22 stone steps of the first flight (each just short of 8 feet wide and 4 to 5 inches high) have survived. This first flight rose to a landing in the south. From this landing a second flight of stairs (this time of wood) mounted in the opposite direction (westwards) to a second landing on the same level as the Vestibule. The royal apartments were located north-west of the Megaron. All that has remained are the foundation walls of one corner of a small room with a red coloured floor. This room was taken as the bathroom in which Clytemnestra murdered Agamemnon.

At the highest point on the Acropolis we can still see the foundations of an Hellenistic Temple which was built over the remains of an earlier temple dating from the 7th century B. C. This Temple — possibly in honour of the goddess Athena — had its axis running from north to south.

If we now descend eastwards from the Acropolis, we come upon another group of foundation walls of which the most important are known as the "Artist's House" and the "House of Columns". The "Artist's House" had two rows of well-constructed rooms — perhaps this was in fact the eastern section of the Palace. Its name derives from the remains of ivory, precious stones and gold that were found here during the excavations.

The "House of Columns" lies to the east and was so dubbed because of the foundations of 10 columns that have survived in an impressive quadrangular court. In this part of the building complex there was also a Megaron.

THE SECRET CISTERN (plate 73)

We continue our descent north-eastwards and arrive thus at the final extension of the Cyclopean walls which was undertaken in the 13th century B. C. This extension was to enclose within the fortifications the secret subterranean cistern which was also built around this same time. This was necessary for the simple reason that the three Mycenaean wells on the Acropolis and the cisterns in which rainwater was collected were not enough to ensure an adequate water supply for the defenders in the event of siege.

This underground cistern is a magnificent witness to the state of Mycenaean technology. Its entrance was in the north-eastern corner.

The high-vaulted cistern ("scissor arch") reaches a depth of 52 feet 6 inches, to which one descends by 99 steps. These steps ran under the Cyclopean wall and then led north-westwards to a landing where they descended in the opposite direction to a second landing. A further 60 steps led north-east to the well, which is a little over 16 feet deep. The cistern and some of the steps had a waterproof finish to prevent any of the water seeping away. A subterranean channel brought the water from a spring located to the north which has since dried up. This was not the

Perseia Fountain. On account of the pitch darkness, visitors wanting to descend should take a powerful torch or flashlight with them.

East of the Secret Cistern, there is a narrow Sally Port cutting through the wall to north. This enabled the defenders to launch a suprise attack from the rear on besiegers.

Next to the Sally Port there is another Cistern dating from Hellenistic times. Opposite, a large passageway pierced the southern wall to lead to a terrace which served as an observation post. To the north-east there are also the foundations of a number of other buildings. A path leads along the northern wall to the North Postern Gate.

THE NORTH POSTERN GATE (plate 74)

This northern gateway was built at a later period than the Lion Gate. In form it is roughly the same, except that it is smaller and does not have a relieving triangle ornamented with sculpture. In front of it, there was a narrow court and a tower which made it easy for the guards to ward off an attack. The visitor should now follow in a westerly direction the path that runs along the line of the northern wall (below the northern side of the Palace) until he arrives back at the Lion Gate.

THE GRAVES

From the 19th to the 17th centuries B. C. the dead were buried in simple graves that took the form of a shaft or pit. They were square graves sunk in the earth and lined with vertical stone slabs. The dead were also buried in hollow out rock. This is the earliest form of burial and such graves are known as pit or cist graves. From the 17th century B. C. onwards this type of grave was further elaborated and also used for royal burials. The pits were dug very deep and small walls were erected at the sides on which posts were compactly laid which were then covered in turn with stone slabs. These are known as shaft graves.

Six royal shaft graves were discovered in Grave Circle A (cf. above) and a further 14 in Grave Circle B outside the Acropolis.

Some of the graves of Grave Circle B are of earlier date (turn of the 17th/16th century), whereas those of Grave Circle A are to be placed in the 16th century.

From the 17th century onwards it was the custom to place valuable funerary offerings alongside the deceased in the royal graves. Two other types of graves found in Mycenae are the chamber tombs and the tholos or beehive tombs. The chamber tombs were family graves and are of earlier date than the tholos graves. Both types have in common: a passageway or dromos, an entrance and a chamber. Ordinary mortals were laid to rest in the chamber tombs and kings in the tholos tombs.

The Chamber Graves

The method of construction was as follows: a passageway was driven into the side of a hill until it reached a length of 40 to 100 feet. This was then widened into an entrance which led to the chamber. The latter was dug out of the earth or out of not-too-solid rock. The chamber was often, though not always, quadrangular or circular in form and was some 20 feet long, 18 feet wide and 21 to 23 feet high. The dead were laid on the floor of these subterranean graves and the funerary offerings then placed around them. Finally the hillside entrance was closed with stones. The dead of the same family were laid in the same grave. When there was no more room on the floor, the skeletons were piled in the corners to make more space for other deceased members of the family. The hills around Mycenae are riddled with such graves, many of which lie to the right and left of the road which leads to the present-day village of Mycenae.

The Tholos or Beehive Tombs

The tholos or beehive tomb is a further development and elaboration of the chamber tomb. They are more dignified and were intended only for royal personages. In Mycenae 9 such graves have been found: they consist of a passageway or dromos, an entrance or "doorway" and the tholos.

A. J. B. Wace, the English archaeologist, arranged the tholos graves chronologically into three periods on the basis of their main characteristics. The oldest tombs are those of Cyclopeios, of Epano Phournos and of Aegisthus: they were built around 1510—1460 B. C. During this period the tholos was constructed of small unhewn stones, the entrance of somewhat bigger stones. The large stone which serves as the lintel is not curved inside, the passageway is not lined with stones and there is no relieving triangle over the entrance.

The tombs of Panagia, Kato Phournos and of the Lion are assigned to the second period. They were constructed between 1460 and 1400. The tholos and the opening are built of rectangular stones. The upper section of the entrance is now formed to match the shape of the vault of the tholos and has a relieving triangle.

In the third period we have the tombs of the Genii, of Atreus and of Clytemnestra. They date from the period 1400—1300 B. C. and are the most perfect of their kind. Passageway, entrance and tholos are built of well-hewn, rectangular stones. However, the names assigned to them do not correspond in reality to those buried within them.

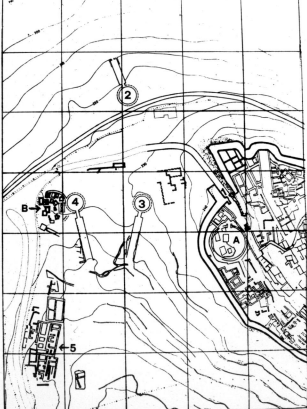

GRAVES

A Grave Circle A B Grave Circle B 1 The Lion Gate 2 Lion Tholos Tomb 3 Tholos Tomb of Aegisthus 4 Tholos Tomb of Clytemnestra 5 Four Houses on the Modern Road

When the visitor goes out through the Lion Gate, he can view the three tomb types just described within the archaeological zone.

On the way to the exit, and a little lower than the path, we come to the Lion Tomb (second period).

The roof of the tholos has collapsed. The Tomb of Aegisthus, one of the earliest (c. 1500 B. C.) lies on the left of the path and to the west of the Lion Gate. Further west still lies the socalled Tomb of Clytemnestra. It dates from the third period and, in Professor Mylonas' view, was the last of the tholos tombs and was constructed around 1220 B. C. It was completely unknown until the year 1809 when it was accidentally discovered by the inhabitants of Chervation (the present-day Mycenae) as they were laying a new water line. The Turks demolished part of the tholos and removed its contents. The Greek Office of Monument Conservation and Restoration reconstructed the tholos in 1951.

The Hellenistic theatre that was built over it shows that the tomb was unknown at that time, too. Of this theatre only a few seats have survived. Of the 9 tholos or beehive tombs, 3 of them are located within the archaeological zone, as described. The Treasury of Atreus is near the road; it will be the last structure we shall visit. The rest are situated on the west side of Panagitsa Hill.

GRAVE CIRCLE B

Not far from and to the west of the Tomb of Clytemnestra lies Grave Circle B, which was excavated by Joannis Papadimitriou and G. Mylonas during the years 1952—1955. The circle was accidentally discovered when restoring the Tomb of Clytemnestra in 1951.

The enclosing wall around Grave Circle B was built of large stones and was 4 feet high and 5 feet thick. A little less than 60 feet of the northern section of the wall has survived. The circle was 92 feet in diameter. Inside the circle, 24 graves were laid bare and each is designated by a letter of the Greek alphabet. 14 of them are royal shaft graves and the rest of them are hewn out of the rock.

Among the graves of this circle, grave P is the most outstanding because of its size and mode of construction. It was built around 1450 B. C. and is unique in the whole of Greece. Within a shaft grave (23 x 10 feet) a chamber-shaped tomb with entrance and chamber was constructed of ordinary stone. The entrance is 8 feet 6 inches long and 4 feet wide and the chamber is a little over 8 feet 7 inches deep. The walls incline at the top to form a sort of gable. The roof of the entrance consisted of a horizontal stone slab.

The biggest tomb in Grave Circle B is tomb Γ. It is 12 feet 6 inches in length and 9 feet 3 inches in width. Tomb Ξ is smaller and measures 9 feet in length, just under 6 feet in width and 6 feet 6 inches in height.

The funerary offerings which were found here were not quite of such great value as in Grave Circle A. But they also found here gold and silver beakers, swords of bronze, small swords, ear-rings, rings and diverse other things. A tiny bust of a Mycenaean, less than 1/2 inch in size, which is engraved in a mosaic stone of amethyst, stands out because of its fine workmanship. Also remarkable is a small bottle of rock crystal wrought in the form of a goose.

OTHER RUINS

South of Grave Circle B and near the road, there was once a group of four buildings. The northernmost of them is known as the "House of Shields" on account of the pieces of ivory found there in which shields were engraved in the form of a figure 8.

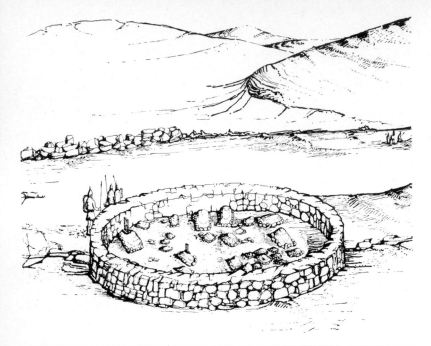

Reconstruction of Grave Circle B (By A. Voyiatzis)

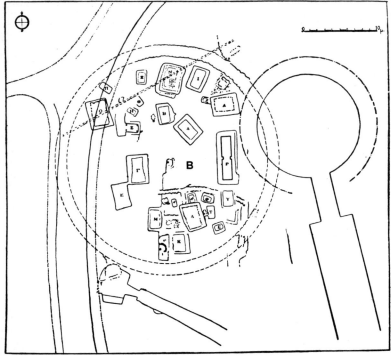

Plan of the Grave Circle B (By D. Theocharis)

The "House of the Oil Merchant" lies a little further south. Its name stems from the 11 containers which were found here in an underground chamber and in which oil was stored. They stood 3 feet 3 inches high and were placed in a row against the wall, separated from one another by a small wall so that each stood firm.

Farther south still lay the "House of the Sphinx". It was so called because of the plate of ivory found here in which various sphinx figures were incised. West of the House of the Oil Merchant is the West House. Here a lot of tablets were found inscribed with linear B script.

The building complex was destroyed by fire in the 13th century B. C.

During the Geometric Period it served as a cemetery; during the Hellenistic Age as a habitation.

THE TREASURY OF ATREUS (plates 87, 88)

The Treasury of Atreus lies a little outside the archaeological zone, to the right of the road that leads to the village of Mycenae.

When Pausanias visited Mycenae in the 2nd century B. C., the people of his day were still of the opinion that the tholos graves were treasure-houses, with the result that the Tomb of Atreus still bears this designation today (the same applies to the socalled Treasury of Minyas at Orchomenus, Boeotia).

The Treasury of Atreus or, as it is more generally known, the Tomb of Agamemnon is architecturally the most perfect monument of its kind. It dates from the same period as the Lion Gate. It was burrowed into the eastern side of Panagitsa Hill. Its dromos is just short of 40 feet long; it is reveted with well-hewn stones in carefully laid courses. The walls follow the natural inclination of the hill as far as the entrance, which looks east. The façade is 34 feet in height. The entrance to the tomb measures 17 feet 8 inches in height and a little under 9 feet in width at the bottom and 8 feet in width at the top. This narrowing towards the top makes the entrance look still more impressive, still mightier. Above the entrance are two large stone slabs, the upper section of the doorway.

The dimensions of the huge monolith employed as an architrave are enormous: 29 feet 6 inches long, 19 feet 6 inches wide and 4 feet thick! It is estimated to be 120 tonnes in weight! Inside it conforms to the shape of the tholos.

"Treasury of Atreus" — Reconstruction of the entrance façade (By Alan Wace)

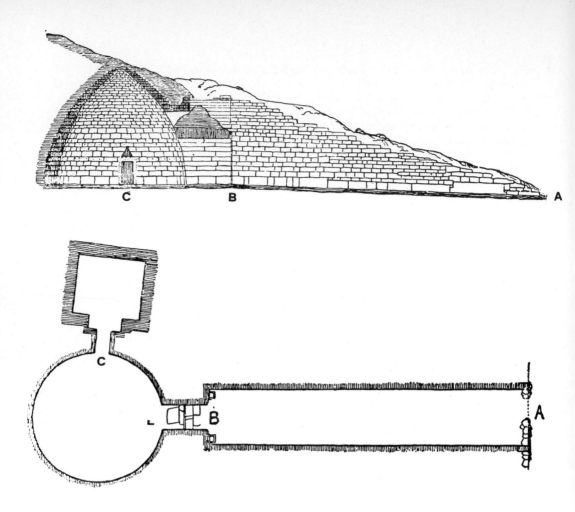

Plan and section of the "Treasury of Atreus" A Entry to the Dromos B Doorway to the Tomb C Tholos
Tomb and entry to the Side Chamber

When the visitor views the monolith from within, then he can only wonder at the skill with which the architect and craftsmen integrated it so perfectly into the overall design of the entrance. The entrance wall is 17 feet thick. A relieving triangle has been employed in the upper section of the doorway. Two large half columns in green stone and with incised ornamentation were placed to the left and right of the exterior entrance and immediately above them were two further half columns which were much smaller but likewise ornamented with inscribed decoration. The relieving triangle was covered with large stones and the space between the two small columns was ornamented with Mycenaean friezes and half-rosettes arranged in horizontal lines. These two half columns can be viewed in the Mycenaean Room of the National Museum, Athens.

A two-winged wooden door stood at the centre of the 17-foot thick wall of the entrance. The tholos itself was just a fraction under 48 feet in diameter and 44 feet high. It was constructed of 33 courses of well-hewn stones laid so as to distribute the load of the structure, i. e. they incline gradually towards the top until they meet at the point of the final stone.

The interior of the entire tholos was decorated with frieze bands and half-rosettes wrought on leaves of bronze. Alongside the main chamber there was a lateral chamber hewn out of the rock and ornamented in a similar fashion.

This second, smaller chamber is found only in the Treasury of Atreus here (otherwise only in the above-mentioned tomb at Orchomenus).

Because there were no funerary gifts found in the Treasury of Atreus and the other tholos tombs, it was extremely difficult to date them exactly. First, both the Treasury and the Lion Gate were assigned to around 1330 B. C. However, the most recent excavations have revealed that both structures were built c. 1250 B. C. This view is also supported by the tradition which has come down to us that this impressive tomb was built during the reign of Atreus for himself and his offspring. Thus, it does indeed look as though it really was the tomb of Atreus and of Agamemnon.

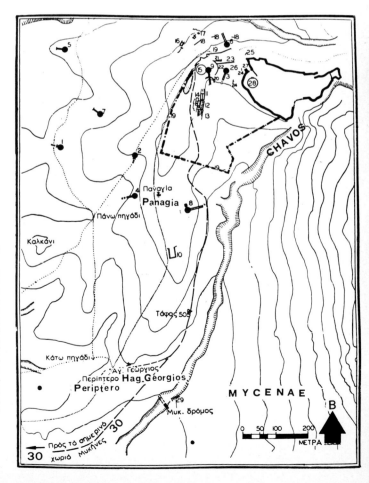

PLAN OF MYCENAE

The Acropolis, the City and the Tholos Tombs (By C. K. Williams)

Tholos Tombs: 1510—1460 B. C. 1 Cyclopean 2 Epano Phournos 3 Of Aegisthos 1460—1400 4 Panagia 5 Kato Phournos 6 Lion Tomb 1400—1300 7 Tomb of the Genii 1400—1300 8 Treasury of Atreus 1220 9 Tomb of Clytemnestra 10 House of Lead vase 11 House of Shields 12 House of the Oil Merchant 13 House of Sphinxes 14 West House 15 Grave Circle B 16 House of the Wine Merchant 17 Petsas' House 18 Hellenistic Walls 19 Hellenistic Walls of the Lower Town 20 Hellenistic Theatre 21 Fountain Perseia 22, 23, 24 Mycenaean Walls 25 Water Channel 26 Prehistoric Cemetery 27 Lion Gate 28 Grave Circle A 29 Sanctuary of Agamemnon 30 Street to Mycenae Village

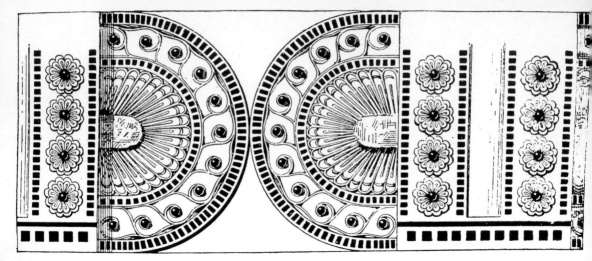

The Kyanos Frieze

TIRYNS

To get to Tiryns from Mycenae, the visitor is recommended to drive through the town of Argos and from there in the direction of Nauplia. After 5 miles a road turns off to the left which leads to the entrance of the archaeological zone of Tiryns.

The *Acropolis* of Tiryns is an isolated low ridge of rock which rises only 85 feet above sea-level and some 59 feet above the surrounding plain. Yet, in spite of this, the oldest and most strongly fortified of all the Mycenaean citadels in Greece was built here.

The ridge runs as a long narrow outjut in a north-south direction. It is 985 feet long and varies from roughly 150 to almost 330 feet in width.

Like the hill of Mycenae, this was a site that was already inhabited in early historical times, long before the fortifications and the other buildings were constructed. Indeed, German archaeologists, when excavating the summit of the Acropolis, uncovered a circular structure which dates back to the proto-Helladic period (c. 2500 B. C). This edifice was almost 90 ft across. It must have been an early palace or a guard house.

The Acropolis of Tiryns was built in three stages. During the first phase (c. 1400 B. C.) the palace was built on the highest point of the ridge, at the centre of the southern part where it is at its widest. During the second phase (1300—1250 B. C.) an extensive Cyclopean wall was constructed in a northerly direction to enclose the central section.

A second Cyclopean wall, along the east side of the hill, made the citadel impregnable along that side, too. The Gate was transferred at this time to the north. During the third and last phase (1250—1200 B. C.) the Acropolis was given its final form. A Cyclopean wall built northwards completed the fortification system so that the citadel was protected on all sides. The wall was now over 2377 feet long, was from nearly 15 to over 58 (!) feet thick, or, on average, 24 feet 6 inches thick (= its thickness along the south side). It has a maximum height of 24 feet 7 inches. It was during this period that the impressive palace with its propylaea, the Great Gate, the south-west hidden stairway to the exit and the galleries were built.

On the east side, a steep ramp led outside the walls to the Main Entrance. This ramp followed the line of the wall from north to south and was only 15 feet wide. It was however of immense strategic importance. On the one hand, it rendered a massed attack impossible; on the other, attackers were exposed during the whole of the ascent, so that they could easily be beaten off by the guards on the walls. The Main Entrance was roughly 8 feet wide, extremely narrow. It led to a passageway which was likewise very narrow and enclosed on both sides by lofty walls. This passageway led to the right (northwards) to the lower northern Acropolis and to the south to the Great Gate of the Upper Acropolis.

THE GREAT GATE (plate 93)

In its dimensions and method of construction, the Great Gate is extremely similar to the Lion Gate at Mycenae, so much so in fact that archaeologists have dubbed it the " sister " of the latter. It is said to have been built by the same architect.

All that has survived of the Great Gate is its lower section, 13 feet long and 4 feet 9 inches wide. The western section of the Gate was 10 feet 6 inches high. A two-winged wooden door, six inches thick, hung in the gateway (9 feet 4 inches wide). The upper section and the relieving triangle have unfortunately not survived — perhaps there was a relief of lions on the latter as well. The total height of the Gate was a fraction over 26 feet. Behind it there were two walls which bore a wooden roof (14 feet long). If one then proceeds in a southerly direction, one comes to a narrow court, on the east side of which once stood a gallery of which only the foundations have survived. Below this there is another gallery with gabled vaulting (plate 101). This was constructed of large stones and on its east side there were 6 rooms, quadrangular in shape. In ascending now to the upper court, the visitor arrives at the impressive main propylaea of the Palace. There were two galleries to the east and west and two wooden columns. Between the two galleries there was a wall pierced by a doorway that led to a large courtyard. In the west gallery a door led to the apartments and the small megaron of the queen.

From the southern corner of the great courtyard, one walks past some foundation walls and comes to a stairway that leads to the vaulted south gallery within the wall (plate 102). The only difference between this and the east gallery described above is that it has only 5 rooms.

To the south-west of the wall, near the south gallery, there was a tower with two rooms.

On the northern side of the great courtyard there were two rooms for the guards and a small propylaea similar to the main one. On passing through this latter, the visitor enters the inner court of the Megaron. This had three colonnades along the east, west and south sides. There was a large circular altar next to the small propylaea. The floor of the court was strewn with white powder. The Megaron, the most imposing structure of the Palace, stood at its north side.

THE MEGARON (plates 97, 100)

The Megaron at Tiryns is the most splendid and best preserved of all the palaces. It measured 82 feet in length and 41 feet in width. Its portico had 2 columns and walls ornamented with 7 plates of the finest alabaster which were in turn decorated with reliefs, half-rosettes and lapis lazuli incrustations. Today scholars are of the almost unanimous opinion that this lapis lazuli is the Homeric " kyanos " (cyanogen = dark-blue colour) that was part of the magnificent ornamentation of the palace of Alcinous.

Three doors in the northern wall of the portico led into an anteroom situated between the portico and the Megaron. Through it one came to the Megaron, the most important room of the Palace. It measured some 35×32 feet and its interior was finely ornamented. A circular hearth stood at the centre. Around it were 4 columns to carry the roof. The throne stood at the right of the entrance in the eastern wall. The plastered floor was divided into painted squares in imitation of the panels of a carpet. These were ornamented with representations of octapuses, dolphins and network. The walls were covered with paintings of hunting scenes, of women in a waggon drawn by horses, of ladies of the court in luxurious garments, of herds of deer, of sphinx forms and other motifs. Dominating all, however, was a representation of the royal hunt in which numerous courtiers also took part.

A detail shows a boar running for its life to escape the attacking hounds but already wounded by the spears of the hunters (plate 99). Not only men but women as well take part in the hunt. Almost at the centre of the Megaron, near the foundations of the columns, a foundation wall has survived that was part of an ancient temple erected around 650 B. C. A temple already stood here c. 750 B. C. but it was destroyed by an earthquake. It was dedicated to the goddess Hera, the patron deity of the Argolic Plain.

A door led westward from the anteroom between portico and Megaron through a zigzagging corridor to the *royal apartments.*

Special among the royal rooms is the bathroom with a floor of highly polished stone pierced with holes for the water to drain off.

The same corridor continues along the northern wall of the Megaron and ends on the east side in the court leading to the queen's megaron. This was in the same style as that of the king, except that it was smaller and simpler. It had a portico, a square hearth and a place for the throne. There were stairways to the next storey in the east near the queen's megaron and to the west of the king's Megaron. A further stairway led northwards down to the lower court which formed the Central Acropolis. Here were the workshops and the dwellings of the various craftsmen and workmen. A huge Cyclopean wall separated the Central from the Lower Acropolis which lay to the north.

THE SECRET STAIRWAY (plate 94)

An exit led westwards from the court to the western hidden Stairway, which is regarded as the most perfect example of the fortification architecture of Mycenaean times and as one of the most significant structures of ancient Greece. Since there was no water on the Acropolis and the nearest spring was over 260 feet outside the walls, this hidden stairway was built to protect those fetching water. It was built along the west side of the Cyclopean wall. A sickle-shaped wall enclosed the stairway with its 80 steps. The entrance was extremely narrow on the outside of the wall and then widened out like a funnel on the inside. Enemy troops that ventured as far forth as this external entrance could easily be picked off by the guards. And even if they managed to get further up the steps, they would not be able to proceed farther because there was a pitfall or trap built into the upper section of the stairway: this was an open space under which there was a 23-foot-deep well covered by a large board; as soon as the guards noticed that the enemy soldiers were standing on this, they operated a lever and both soldiers and board went hurtling down into the well.

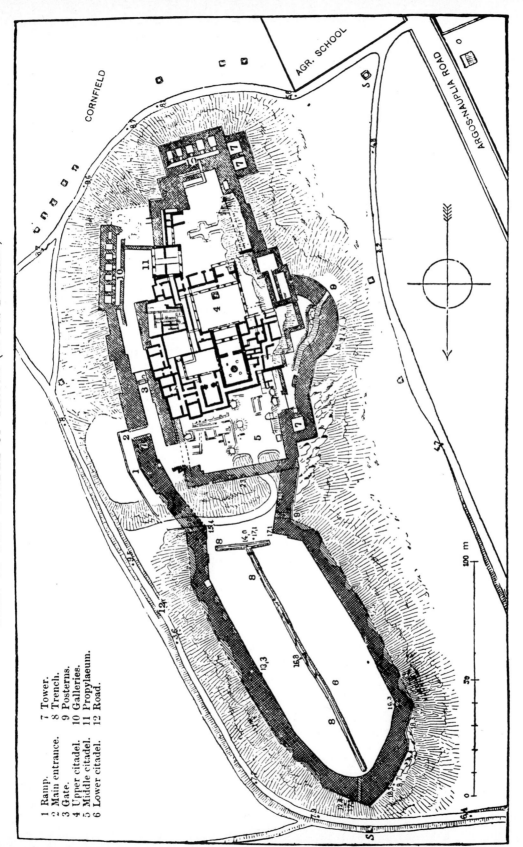

PLAN OF THE CITADEL OF TIRYNS (BY DR. DÖRPFELD)

1 Ramp.
2 Main entrance.
3 Gate.
4 Upper citadel.
5 Middle citadel.
6 Lower citadel.
7 Tower.
8 Trench.
9 Posterns.
10 Galleries.
11 Propylaeum.
12 Road.

AGR. SCHOOL

ARGOS-NAUPLIA ROAD

CORNFIELD

100 m

39

The Lower Acropolis was built on the northern section of the ridge of Tiryns. Its dimensions were similar to those of the Central and Upper Acropolis, and Cyclopean walls enclosed it, too. In times of peace it was not inhabited. However, when there was danger of war, the inhabitants of the town below fled to find shelter within its walls. Since the most important thing in times of siege was the water supply, they built at the same time as the wall two subterranean galleries which led beneath the wall to a spring. In this way they could fetch water without danger. The galleries are similar in construction to the secret underground cistern at Mycenae (gabled vaulting).

LEGEND AND HISTORY

Legend tells us that the first king of Tiryns was called Proetus, a twin brother of Acrisius and an uncle of Perseus. As the two brothers did not get on well with one another, Acrisius expelled Proetus when he became king of Argos. Proetus found refuge at the court of Iobates, king of Lycia, who gave him his daughter, Antia, in marriage, helped him to return to Argos and compelled Acrisius to confer on him the throne of Tiryns.
Proetus then sent to Lycia for the Cyclopes and commissioned them to construct fortification walls in order to render the Acropolis at Tiryns impregnable. On his death, he was succeeded by his son, Megapenthes. When Perseus became king of Argos, he exchanged thrones with his cousin: Megapenthes became king of Argos, Perseus of Tiryns. Then, as we have already seen, Perseus founded Mycenae and fortified it with enclosing walls. He was at the same time king of Tiryns. His offspring Sthenelus, Amphitryon and Eurystheus were kings of both places, too.
Alcmene, the wife of King Amphitryon, bore the famous hero Heracles after Zeus had come to her disguised as her husband. Heracles then became the servant of King Eurystheus for whom he carried out his famous 12 labours.
When the kingship of Mycenae passed from the descendants of Perseus to Atreus and his line, the latter also reigned over Tiryns.
Homer mentions that men from Tiryns " mighty of ramparts " also took part in the siege of Troy with other contingents from Achaea. Their commander was Diomedes with the voice of thunder; he was a son of Tydeus and led a fleet of 80 ships. After the conquest of Troy, Tiryns was never again mentioned in legends or the written sources. Archaeological excavations and research have shown that Tiryns was at the height of its power around 1200 B. C. Shortly afterwards a large part of the Palace was destroyed in a conflagration, but then quickly rebuilt. After the coming of the Dorians, Tiryns continued to be inhabited but it had lost the splendour of former times. At the close of the Geometric Age and in the early Archaic Period, the Megaron was converted into a Temple of Hera. This Temple was not so wide as the Megaron and had no colonnades. The Dorian migration brought about the decline of Mycenae and Tiryns, whereas it initiated a period of rising prosperity for Argos.
According to Herodotus (Book 9, Ch. 28), a small contingent of 400 inhabitants of Mycenae and Tiryns took part in the Battle of Plataea against the Persians (479 B. C.). The Argives, who had not taken part, destroyed Tiryns in the year 468 B. C. out of envy and jealousy at the fame their part in the battle had brought them. The inhabitants of Tiryns left the town and settled in the region of Porto Heli. Their new town they called Alieis or Alike. When Pausanias visited Tiryns in the 2nd century, he was so impressed by the Cyclopean walls there that he compared them to the pyramids in Egypt. He remarked that they were to be numbered among the

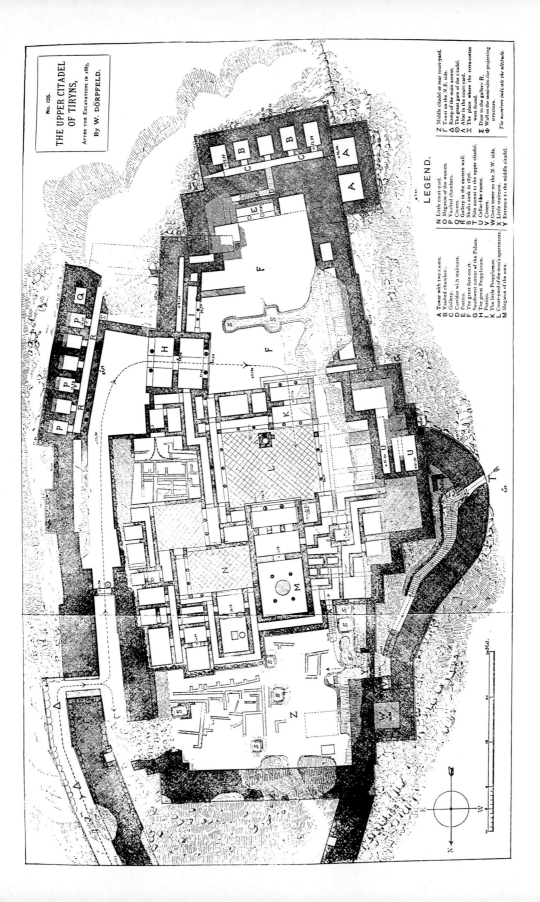

No. 125.

THE UPPER CITADEL
OF TIRYNS,

AFTER THE EXCAVATIONS IN 1885,

By W. DÖRPFELD.

LEGEND.

A Tower with two rooms.
B Vaulted chamber.
C Gallery.
D Corridor with staircase.
E Portico.
F The great fore-court.
G Southwest corner of the Palace.
H The great Propylaeum.
I Portico.
K The little Propylaeum.
L Court-yard of the men's apartments.
M Megaron of the men.

N Little court-yard.
O Megaron of the women.
P Vaulted chambers.
Q Cistern.
R Gallery in the eastern wall.
S Shafts sunk in 1876.
T Side ascent to the upper citadel.
U Cellar-like rooms.
V Cistern.
W Great tower on the N.W. side.
X Little staircase.
Y Entrance to the middle citadel.

Z Middle citadel or rear court-yard.
Γ Tower on the N.E. side.
Δ Ramp of the main ascent.
Θ The great gate of the citadel.
Λ Altar in the court-yard.
Ξ The place where the terra-cottas were found.
Σ Door to the gallery R.
Φ Wall on the semi-circular projecting structure.

The numbers indicate the altitude.

greatest and most remarkable edifices of the world and that a pair of mules would not even be able to move even one of the smallest of the walls' stones.

THE EXCAVATIONS

The first to dig in Tiryns, but on a small scale, were Friedrich Thiersch and Alexander Rangavis in 1831. Heinrich Schliemann started his activities in 1876 and it was he and Wilhelm Dörpfeld who carried out the first real excavation of Tiryns in 1884/85. Dörpfeld exercised the greatest care in uncovering the entire Palace complex. The German Archaeological Institute in Athens under Dörpfeld then continued the digs up to 1929. After World War II, the Greek Archaeological Institute took up the excavations again. The archaeologist N. Verdelis carried out digs in the northern part of the Lower Acropolis and laid bare two subterranean galleries. The Greek Office of Monument Conservation and Restoration is attempting a reconstruction along the southern and western sections of the wall. The German Archaeological Institute began its investigations at Tiryns again in 1965.

*

NAUPLION

The beautiful and picturesque town of Nauplion, today the capital of the nomôs (department) of Argolis, lies south of Tiryns. It is built on the northern slope of a great crag which protrudes out into the Bay of Argolis to form a small peninsula.

Lerna, the oldest town of Argolis, is situated exactly opposite Nauplion on the other side of the gulf.

Just outside the harbour of Nauplion there is a tiny island on which a small Venetian castle still stands. This is the island of Bourtzi, the pride and jewel of Nauplion. It lies like a ship at anchor out in the bay, at times reflected in the still, blue waters of the harbour, at others riding like some proud ship in the bay with the waves breaking against its bows.

Above and to the east of Nauplion rises the hill of Palamidi on the summit of which is situated the renowned Venetian castle with the 999 steps. Even today Nauplion still bears all the marks of the various epochs and of the different conquerors who at times ruled over the town.

Narrow lanes and alleyways, old houses and various styles of churches with their picturesque towers are typical. The Last Supper in the metropolitan church is an excellent copy of Leonardo da Vinci's famous picture in Milan; it is the work of D. Georgantas of Tinos. The Venetian edifice that today houses the Museum, the Law Courts, the Chamber of Deputies, the first University in Greece, the squares and gardens, and the two hills overlooking the town, Palamidi and Acronauplia, give the town a refined air all of its own that makes it unique among the towns of the Peloponnesus.

From mythical times down to the present day, Nauplion has always had an important role to play in maritime trade and commerce. From its harbour Mycenaean ships, laden heavy with goods, set sail to ply the entire Mediterranean and bring their wares as far afield as Egypt. Today ships are loaded with thousands of tons of oranges and lemons bound for a whole number of European countries.

Both legend and tradition assign the honour of founding Nauplion to Nauplius, the son of Poseidon and Amymone, one of the daughters of Danaus. Nauplius was a celebrated seafarer. He sailed from Euboea, where he was born, and so came to Argolis. There, on the rocky crag which extends like a cape out into the eastern corner of the Bay of Argolis, he built a city which he named Nauplia. He enclosed it within Cyclopean walls, erected a temple in honour of Poseidon, his father, and founded an association of maritime towns with its centre at Calauria (island of Poros).

The first inhabitants of Nauplia were Egyptians brought by Danaus. Five generations later another Nauplius, a descendant of the first, a seafarer and astronomer of great renown, took part in the expedition of the Argonauts. He is credited with discovering the constellation of the Little Bear as a means of navigation.

Nauplius had a son by Clymene, a daughter of Atreus or Catreus. This son, Palamedes, was an astronomer and physician and the inventor of weights and measures, the light-house, the dice, as also four of the Greek letters: Z, Π, Φ, X.

He also took part in the campaign against Troy, but, as he was wiser and more discerning than Odysseus, the king of Ithaca, the latter was jealous of him. In order to rid himself of Palamedes, he contrived with Diomedes and Agamemnon to make it appear that Palamedes was a friend of Priam and had accepted a sum of gold to betray them. Thus was Odysseus able to incite the army, so that Palamedes was stoned to death.

Before he was done to death, Palamedes cried, " Unhappy truth, you die before me ". When Nauplius heard of the tragic death of his son, he determined to avenge himself on the Achaeans who were returning home as victors.

He had a huge fire lit on Capherus, the rocky Cape of Euboea, the present-day Cavo Doro, which the Achaeans would be passing on their way home. When they arrived there, they believed that the fire was intended to signal the presence of sheltering bays; their ships ran on to the rocks, where they were smashed to pieces. However, when Nauplius learnt that Odysseus, who was really responsible for the death of his son, had not perished in this trap, he threw himself from the cape into the sea and drowned. The lofty rock which dominates Nauplion was given the name Palamidi.

The tragic story of Palamedes and Nauplius was the source of inspiration for the tragedians Aeschylus, Sophocles and Euripides, and they wrote several tragedies which took the story as their theme. Nothing has survived of these tragedies.

HISTORY

Nauplia was founded towards the close of the third millennium and remained inhabited and independent until the year 678 B. C. when it was destroyed by Damocratida, the king of Argos. The inhabitants sought refuge in Methone. Later the Argives dwelt in the town and transformed it into the harbour of Argos. In the settlement of Pronoia at Nauplion a whole series of graves have been uncovered that prove that there was a Mycenaean cemetery there. They also found surgical instruments of bronze which are attributed to Palamedes who, we remember, was said to have been a doctor.

In the fourth century before the Christian era, the polygonal wall was erected. On this the medieval citadel was later built. On his travels, Strabo also visited Nauplia, which he tells us was still inhabited and used as a naval base by the Argives. However, when Pausanias came to Nauplia in the second century A. D., he found the town deserted. He does relate, nevertheless, that there were ruins of the walls and of the Temple of Poseidon, that there were harbours and a spring that was called Canathos. The Argives believed that the goddess Hera bathed once a year in this spring to renew her virginity. He also tells us that a donkey was depicted on a rock there and that this was connected with the following legend: the donkey had eaten the branches of a vine, whereupon the vine bore still more grapes, so that in this way the inhabitants learnt the necessity of pruning their vines.

In 589 A. D. Nauplia was conquered by the Byzantines and named Nauplion. In 879 A. D. it was ruled over by a despot. In 1148 A. D. Leon, the despot of Nauplion, erected the monastery and the church of Zoodochos Pigi. In 1180 A. D. the Byzantine Emperor Manuel Comnenus nominated Theodorus Sguros ruler of the town. In 1189 it was made the seat of a bishop. In 1204 it fell to the Franks under Boniface Montferrat and Godfrey Vilharduin. The Franks were now stationed in one of the two citadels on Acronauplia, whereas the other remained in Greek hands.

In 1212 both Nauplion and Argos became a fief of Otto de la Roche, Grand Duke of Athens, and remained under the sovereignty of the Franks for more than a century. In the year 1389 it was conquered by the Venetians who transformed it into the most powerful fortress in Greece. In the fortresses which they constructed at Methone and Corone they were able to repel many Turkish sieges. However, in the year 1540, the Venetians were compelled to hand over Nauplion to the Turks, with whom they had signed a treaty. In the 16th and 17th centuries, Nauplion was the capital of Turkish Morea. In 1686, the Venetian Morosini took Nauplion and fortified Palamidi according to the latest principles of fortification. He also erected the walls of Acronauplia and of Bourtzi. The building works were completed in

44

1714. Just one year later Morea was subjugated by the Turks. The fall of Nauplion sealed the fate of the entire Peloponnesus. On 20 November 1822 the Greeks, with Staikos Staikopoulos at their head, took Palamidi with the consequence that the town itself was surrendered to them on 1 December 1822. On 7 January 1823 Kapodistrias (Count Capo d'Istria), the first president of the Greek Republic, landed at Nauplion. However, he was assassinated by the Mavromichales brothers as he entered the church of St Spiridon on 27 September 1828.

On 25 January 1833, Otto, first king of Greece and son of King Ludwig I of Bavaria, arrived at Nauplion. In September of the following year King Otto transferred his residence from Nauplion to Athens which was made the new capital of the Greek kingdom. During Otto's stay at Nauplion, a number of public buildings were erected in the neoclassical style which are still standing today.

One of the most important historical buildings in Nauplion is the two-storey edifice on Syndagma (Constitution) Square, which was constructed in 1713 as a storehouse for the Venetian fleet. It has been a museum since 1930. Within it, prehistoric and Mycenaean finds from the area around Nauplia, from Mycenae, Tiryns, Dendra (Midea), Asine, Prosymna and elsewhere (plates 107, 108, 109, 110, 111, 112) are on view. Outstanding among the many remarkable finds is a suit of armour that was discovered by the archaeologist N. Verdeli in a tomb at Dendra in 1960. It dates from c. 1450 B. C. and confirms what Homer said when he refers in the Iliad to the Achaeans wearing armour.

BOURTZI

On the tiny island on which stood the Byzantine church of Aghii Theodori, a small citadel was built in 1471 to protect the harbour. This lofty octogonal fortress is known as the Bourtzi of Nauplia. The small semicircular towers were for cannon. From 1930—1970 it served as a hotel.

PALAMIDI (plates 113—116)

Morosini was the first to think of fortifying Palamidi. The fortress of Palamidi consists of eight fortified bastions which are linked together. Originally they had Venetian names; today they are known by their Greek names: Aghios Andreas, the highest, Phokion, Themistokles, Epameinondas, Leonidas and Achilleas. On the centre of Palamidi is the small church of St Andrew and the Koloktroni prison, a small cell hewn out of the rock. It was in this prison that the Greeks held old Kolokotroni captive, who had been convicted of high treason. After 11 months' imprisonment he was pardoned by King Otto. A recently built asphalt road now leads up to the summit of Palamidi. Here stands the monument of the " Bavarian Lion ", which was erected in honour of the Bavarians who died here of typhus (1833/34).

A road leading off to the left before we reach the gate of the fortress takes us to the Karathon coast, one of the most magnificent around Nauplia.

From the summit of Palamidi the visitor is granted one of the most beautiful experiences: a view of Acronauplia, Nauplia, Bourtzi and the Gulf of Argolis and the green Argolic plain.

*

EPIDAURUS

Some 18 ¹/₂ miles north-east of Nauplion lies the sanctuary of Asclepius in ancient Epidaurus. The archaeological zone at Epidaurus is very different from the other archaeological regions that we have so far described.

In ancient Corinth the majority of the ruins that have been laid bare by the archaeologists date from Roman times.

Mycenae and Tiryns were fortified cities and each had an acropolis, the most accomplished fortification works of prehistoric times, so that have come down to us as the sites of warlike and martial peoples. In contrast, the sanctuary of Asclepius at Epidaurus always held aloof from war and struggles for power and remained true to its original calling as a place of healing.

It would appear that Nature itself was here fully in tune with the wishes and intentions of the god of healing, for the area around Epidaurus has numerous springs and plentiful supplies of water. This peaceful, joyful and restful region was well endowed with rich flora, with woods and groves, with splendid flowers and medicinal herbs.

In these ideal surroundings, which one would today say had a " psychotherapeutic " and soothing effect on its visitors, the god Asclepius (Aesculapius), the supreme physician, brought healing through the medium of skilled doctors to those who came seeking his help with faith in his powers, as numerous witnesses attest. We should not forget that the ancient peoples assigned supernatural powers to their " gods ", even if these were at times not completely free of human failings. An appeal to them had its " transcendental " effect as in any other religion; confiding prayer brought to suppliants, if not healing, at least new-found strength.

The Asklepieion, which was founded in the period 500—450 B. C., acquired such a reputation that its renown spread far beyond the boundaries of Greece to neighbouring countries.

The Temple, the Abaton, the Tholos, as also the incomparable Theatre were not just built to complement the natural beauty of the sacred enclosure but, above all, to underpin the therapeutic measures with intellectual stimulation and uplifting experiences.

The Theatre at Epidaurus is the largest and most impressive of ancient Greece and is in an excellent state of preservation. It was built in the 4th century B. C. by the architect Polyclitus the Younger of Argos and was unrivalled for its acoustics. It could seat 14,000 (plate 119). Two impressive gateways gave entrance to the theatre (plate 118).

Today the theatre has been restored as far as this was necessary and every year, from June to August, classical tragedies and comedies are performed here and attract thousands of Greek and foreign visitors (plate 122). In the Museum of Epidaurus the visitor can admire the remains of the famous Tholos, another work of Polyclitus, for example a Corinthian capital (plate 121), various votive offerings and inscriptions. In our " Epidaurus " Guide in this same series, we give detailed descriptions of the various buildings in the archaeological zone, of the Theatre, of the finds on view in the Museum, of the sanctuary of Asclepius and the therapeutic methods employed by the priest-physicians to heal the sick. In this volume, a reference to Epidaurus could not be omitted in order to round off the visitor's impressions from a tour of the Argolis, which now draws to a close with a drive back along the new direct route from Epidaurus to Corinth, along which the natural beauty and the magnificent views will be their own reward.

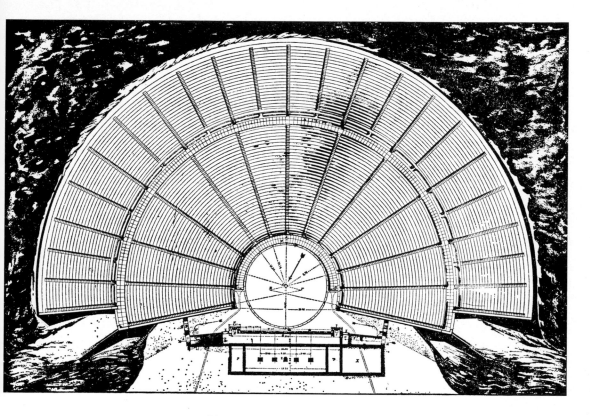

Plan of the Theatre (A. Defrasse)

MYKINAI

MYCENAE   MYCÈNES   MYKENE

61   The Lion Gate   La Porte des Lions   Das Löwentor

Eingang durch das Löwentor

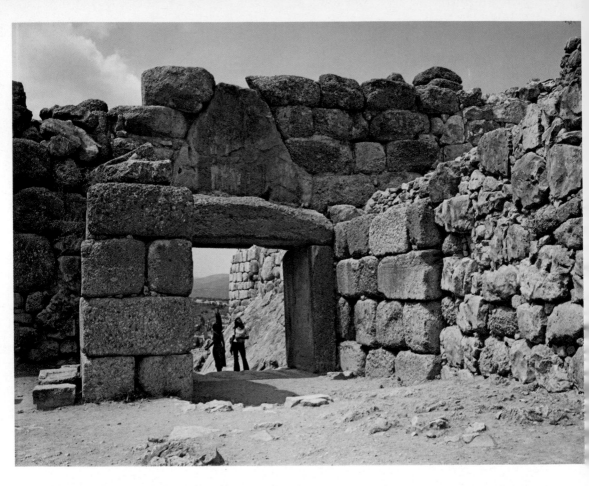

63   The Lion Gate from inside
      La Porte des Lions de l'intérieur
      Das Löwentor von innen

64   The Royal Grave Circle A.
      Le Cercle Royal A.
      Das Rund der Königlichen Gräber A.

65   The '' Warrior Vase ''
      Le « Vase des Guerriers »
      Die „Kriegervase"
      NMA   XIII. s. a. C.

66
The Royal Grave Circle A.
Le Cercle Royal A.
Das Rund der Königlichen Gräber A.

67

The Mycenaean
Acropolis

L'Acropole de My-
cènes

Die Mykenische
Akropolis

69   The Royal Grave Circle A. and the Acropolis
Le Cercle Royal A. et l'Acropole
Das Rund der Königlichen Gräber A. und die Akropolis

70 The Palace. The Great Court
Le Palais Royal. La grande Cour
Der Palast. Der Haupthof

71   The Palace. The Megaron
Le Palais Royal. Le Mégaron
Der Palast. Das Megaron

72   The Tholos Tomb of Klytemnestra
Le Tombeau de Clytemnestre
Das Kuppelgrab der Klytämnestra

73   Passage to the Secret Cistern of Perseia
Passage souterrain menant à la Citerne secrète
Treppe zu der unterirdischen Zisterne Perseia

74 The Postern Gate to the north
La Poterne du Nord
Das Nord-Tor

75   The N. W. angle of the Cyclopean Walls
L'angle N.-O. de l'enceinte cyclopéenne
Die Nordwestecke der Kyklopenmauern

77   Bull' head rhyton in silver and gold
      Rhyton en forme de tête de taureau en argent et o•
      Stierkopf-Rhyton aus Silber und Gold
      No 384 NMA   XVI. s. a. C.

76   Lion-head rhyton in gold
      Rhyton en or en forme de tête de lion
      Löwenkopf-Rhyton aus Gold
      No 273 NMA (Nat. Mus. Ath.)   XVI s. a. C.

78   Gold cup, called '' Nestor's cup ''
      Coupe en or nommée « coupe de Nestor »
      Der sog. „Nestorbecher", aus Gold
      No 412 NMA   XVI. s. a. C.

79   Gold cup from the 4th Grave
      Gobelet en or de la tombe IV
      Goldener Becher aus dem 4. Grab
      No 351 NMA   XVI. s. a. C.

80   Gold diadem from the 3rd Grave
      Diadème en or trouvé dans la 3ème tombe
      Golddiadem aus dem 3. Grab
      No 3,5 NMA   XVI. s. a. C.

81   Gold cup from the 4th Grave
      Coupe en or de la tombe IV
      Goldener Becher aus dem 4. Grab
      No 390 NMA   XVI. s. a. C.

82   Ivory figurine of a sitting woman
         Figurine féminine en ivoire
         Kleine Elfenbeinfigur einer sitzenden Frau
         No 5897 NMA

83   Group of two woman and a child in ivory
         Groupe de deux femmes et un enfant en ivoire
         Zwei Frauen und ein Kind   Elfenbein
         No 7711 NMA

84

Large gold cup from the 5th Grave
Gobelet d'or provenant de la tombe V
Goldener Becher aus dem 5. Grab
No 629 NMA

85 Hexagonal gold-plated wooden box from Shaft-Grave V
Coffret hexagonal en bois recouvert de feuilles d'or
Sechseckige Schachtel mit Goldauflage aus dem 5. Grab
No 808—811 NMA

86
Bronze Dagger blade inlaid in gold and silver
Poignard de bronze incrusté d'or et d'argent
Bronzedolch mit Gold- und Silbereinlagen
No 395 NMA   1600 a. C.

87

The '' Treasury of Atreus ''.
Entrance

Le « Trésor d'Atrée ».
Entré

Das „Schatzhaus des
Atreus". Eingang

Inside of the '' Treasury of Atreus ''
L'intérieur du « Trésor d'Atrée »
Das Innere des „Schatzhauses des Atreus"

89 90   Mycenaean Gold Masks
        Masques en or Mycéniens

Mykenische Gold-Masken
NMA   1580—1550 a. C.

91 Female head in limestone
Tête feminine en calcaire
Weiblicher Kopf   Kalkstein
No 4575 NMA   1200 a. C.

92 The '' Mycenaean Lady ''. Wall-painting
La « Mycénienne ». Fresque
Die „Mykenische Frau". Wandmalerei
NMA

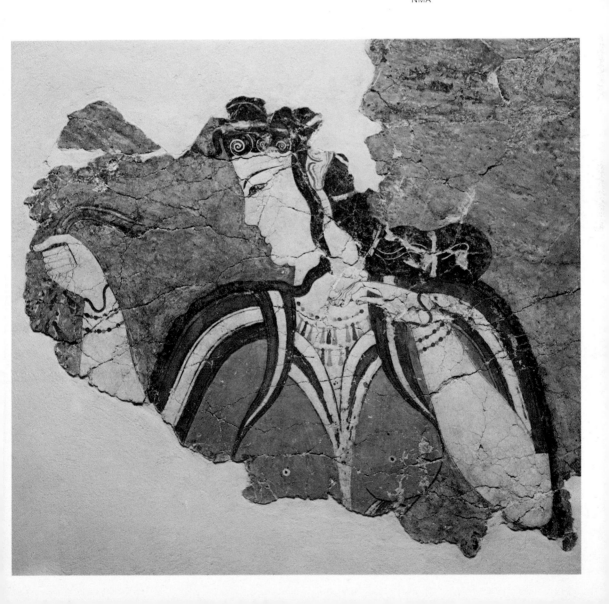

93   Outer Gateway to the Acropolis of Tiryns
     Porte fortifiée de l'enceinte de l'Acropole
     Steintor der Akropolis von Tiryns

TIRYNS

95

The Cyclopean Walls
of Tiryns from the S. W. side

L'enceinte Cyclopéenne de
Tirynthe du côté sud-ouest

Die Kyklopenmauern von
Tiryns (Südwestseite)

96

The Lower Enceinte of the
Fortress

L'enceinte inférieure

Die Unterburg

97 The Palace. The Megaron
Le Palais Royal. Le Mégaron
Der Palast. Das Megaron

98 99
Fragments of wall-paintings from the Palace at Tiryns
Fragments de Fresques du nouveau palais de Tirynthe
Freskomalereien aus dem Palast von Tiryns
NMA   1300—1200 a. C.

100   Entrance to the Megaron
Vestibule du Mégaron
Vorhalle des Megaron

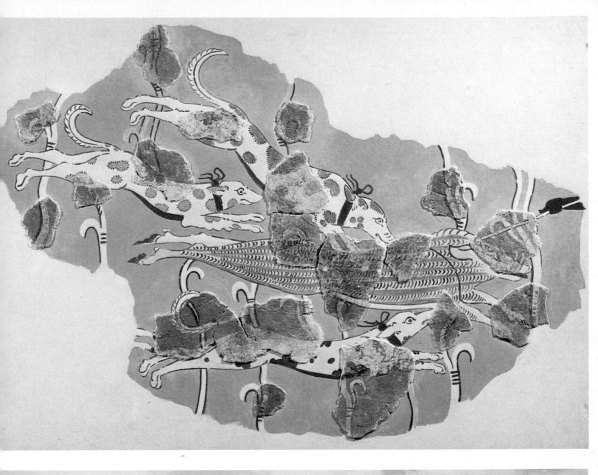

101   The E. Gallery   Les Casemates E.   Südostgalerie

102   The vaulted S. Gallery   Les Casemates S.   Südgalerie

NAUPLION

NAUPLIA   NAUPLIE   NAUPLIA

103   The islet of Bourdzi   L'îlot Bourzi   Die kleine Insel Burzi

| 104 | Nauplia general view | Nauplie, vue générale | Nauplia, Übersicht |
| 105 | The shore of Nauplia | Le rivage de Nauplie | Das Meeresufer von Nauplia |

106   Nauplia from Palamidi   Nauplia, vue générale

Nauplia von der Festung Palamidi aus

107   108
Mycenaean Vases
Vases Mycéniens
Mykenische Vasen

1580—1500 a. C.

NAUPLIA MUSEUM   MUSÉE

109 110
Vases from Asine and Berbati
Vases d'Asiné et de Berbati
Vasen aus Asine und Berbati

AUPLIE   NAUPLIAMUSEUM

112   The "Lord of Asine"
       Le « Lord d'Asine »
       Der „Herr von Asine"
       XII. s. a. C.

113—116
The Fortress of Palamidi
La Citadelle du Palamidi
Die Festung Palamidi über
Nauplia

EPIDAUROS

△ △ 118   The western entrance to the Theatre   L'entrée ouest du théâtre   Das Westtor zum Theater

119   The Theatre   Le Théâtre   Das Theater

THE THOLOS
OF POLYCLEITOS

LA THOLOS
DE POLYCLEITE

DIE THOLOS
DES POLYKLEITOS

120—123

120

Entablature and
doric column

Entablement et
colonne dorique

Gesims und dorische
Säule

121 T H O L O S

Corinthian capital
and column

Chapiteau corinthien
et colonne

Korinthisches Kapitell

122

Performance of a tragedy in the
Theatre of Epidauros

Représentation d'une tragédie
au Théâtre d'Epidaure

Moderne Aufführung einer anti-
ken Tragödie im Theater von
Epidauros

123 THOLOS
Ornaments of the ceiling of the outer colonnade
Ornements des caissons du plafond de la colonnade extérieure
Verzierung der Kassettendecke des äußeren Säulenganges